Best Wishes!

848/999

17

the little way
to get a
lot done

Michael Heppell

17

the little way to get a lot done

ISBN 978-1-8381613-0-9

Published in 2020 by Gloop

A CIP record of this book is available from the British Library.

Printed in the UK by TJ International
Editing and typesetting: www.preparetopublish.com

For Ella Grace

Contents

Introduction

'Mr Heppell.'

'Yes.'

'You have 17 minutes.'

And that's how it started.

It was 5 October 1995, I was in New York and due to meet with Harold Evans (now Sir Harold Evans). He's a publisher – a big name in the world of publishing. I'll always remember that date, as it was the day of the OJ Simpson verdict. I'm sure OJ Simpson remembers that date too.

Harold Evans is a busy bloke, at that time he was president and publisher of Random House, one of the biggest publishers in the world. I patiently waited outside his office while his PA offered me coffee and assured me that Mr Evans wouldn't be too much longer. I knew he was uber important: his assistant had an assistant.

A few minutes later his PA asked if I'd like to go into his office.

And that's when it happened.

As I walked past her desk she calmly but clearly said, 'You have 17 minutes.'

This had never happened to me before. I'd been given:

Quarter of an hour.

5 minutes.

Half an hour.

10 minutes.

Or even: You've got a minute.

But never 17.

When a person values their time so much that their day is broken down by the minute, then you know they're going to get things done.

I've talked about the actual meeting in a couple of my previous books so I won't replay it now.

I remember flying home that night and journaling the details of that extraordinary meeting. I wrote, *His day was so organised that my meeting was scheduled to last for 17 minutes. And it did. To the second.*

Since then I've mainly used 17 as a technique to get things done.

17 is the perfect antidote to my world-class procrastination.

> **17**
>
> **A PRO-crastinator: Someone who is so good at putting things off, they could be a professional**

However, 17 has become much more than just a measure of time. In this book I'm going to introduce you to multiple concepts and ideas, many of which were destined to be linked perfectly to the number 17.

For others, you may need to use your imagination… let's not say square peg/round hole; let's say oval peg.

You'll read about 17%. Where more or less by 17% can have a big impact.

And you'll see 17 as a list. You'll see lots of lists.

And a few other 17 ideas that will inform, educate and entertain.[1]

And like all good books, this one has a promise.

I promise, hand on heart, that if you use the ideas in this book you'll be more productive, focused, creative and effective than you have ever been before. And that's a big promise. Some of my readers are already incredibly effective.

And if that's you – you will get even better.

---

[1] This was the original goal of the BBC – still is. I think they do it rather well.

17 The Number

Some people claim the number 17 has mystical and magical powers. 1 and 7 does make 8 – the luckiest Chinese number.

17 is also a prime number. The super-logical part of my brain loves that – I count as high as possible in prime numbers if I can't get off to sleep. I know – sad.

There are religious and spiritual connotations too. Noah's ark rested on the 17th day of the 7th month. New beginning. Fourth century bishop Augustine of Hippo (cool name for a bishop) suggested that the significance of 153 (St John's 'miraculous catch of fish') was that it's the sum of the digits 1+2+3 and so on to 17, with 17 being the sum of 10, representing the Ten Commandments, and 7, being the number of gifts of the Spirit. And my friend Rev Donald McCorkindale (who supplied these details) suggests the perfect length of sermon to be 17 minutes. But he assures me his are generally shorter!

In numerology 17 is said to be a strong spiritual number associated with creativity and leadership.

So yes, 17 could potentially be a very powerful number.

17 to Set Goals

Using 17 is a brilliant way to set goals too. I'm using my time to write this book – in 17 days. Today is the first day of the 7th month, July 1st. I'm going to write a minimum of 1,000 words a day and aim to have this book published in a maximum of 17 weeks. I'm not sure how much you know about publishing, but 17 weeks, from first word to physical book for sale, is fast.

I often find myself setting crazy deadlines with a caveat of 'why not?'. If I hit it, I move forward faster. If I miss it, I'm wherever I am anyway. If I don't start, I'm going backwards.

That's what I always need... to start.

I'm a professional procrastinator. If procrastination was an Olympic event, I could represent Great Britain and win gold. I wouldn't compete in the next Olympics though, I'd probably go for the one after. Sorry, terrible joke, but closer to the truth that I like to admit.

So, what will you learn in these pages?

Let's start by introducing you to a new way of reading. Only read for 17 minutes and complete one chapter of this book at a time. This is high risk for an author, as everyone reads at different speeds. I'm not going to make each chapter 17 minutes long so I'm going to have to set a few ground rules.

The first is 'flexible is okay'. Your 17 minutes can be, and probably should be, stretched or shrunk when it comes to reading these chapters. Oval peg – round hole, remember?

My cheesy idea, to make each chapter last for around 17 minutes, was for a reason. I once had an Amazon review that described my book as being 'a good loo read'.[2] I took it as a compliment; meaning if you keep the book handy, during a single sitting you could read and learn something.

For some people 17 minutes will be an ambitious length of time to spend reading and even more ambitious length of time on the loo. But I'm going to stick with the premise that you should be able to read a chapter and take actions in 17 minutes.

And you can do this in bed, at your desk, snuggled on the sofa, on your daily commute, or in a plethora of other places.

Take Notes

There should be a law that anyone reading a personal development book should have a pen and paper at hand at all times to make notes. You'll be amazed at how much slips through your overworked brain if you don't catch it on paper.

Okay. If you're ready, then I'm ready. The next and first official chapter introduces the idea of a 17 Minute Sprint. It's a fundamental part of the 17 principle, so make sure you've got a decent amount of time and your notepad and pen ready before you start.

And by decent amount of time I don't expect you to have hours. 17 minutes will be just about right.

---

[2] I normally write by dictating first then editing by keyboard. When I said my book was a good loo read the dictation translated it as 'a good Lou Reed'. I'd settle for that as a review too.

1. 17-Minute Sprints

I can be lazy. Even though I've been described as 'prolific', 'an action man' and 'Mr Energy' (they're the nice ones) I am fundamentally lazy. Yes, given the choice of sitting on a sunbed sipping a G&T or working, those sunbeds and G&Ts win every time. I can do it for days. I have done it for days. But I have clients and friends who are itching to get back to their offices after a few days away from their desks.

I'm also very good at putting things off. Or, more accurately, finding something wonderfully important or distracting to do (shiny thing!) rather than focusing on what I should be doing (non-shiny thing). There's a lot more to come on overcoming procrastination, but I'll write about that later ;)

Welcome to the 17-Minute Sprint

Technically minded people and those involved with pushing projects in high growth businesses understand the importance of a 'sprint'. It's normally two weeks of massive action to formulate, create and test ideas.

Then there's the athletic sprint. Whoosh – 10 seconds to get over the line first.

And then there are my sprints. They always last for... 17 minutes.

I actually considered researching some science to verify my idea that 17 minutes would be the perfect length of time to get something done. In these days of 'The Google' I could probably find something 'sciencey' that proves my theory that 17 minutes is the perfect length of time. But I don't need to. I've tested it, taught it to thousands of people and used it for long enough to know it just works.

And it's so ridiculously simple that you could risk missing the importance of this tool and how significant it could become to your life.

Pause here for dramatic effect…

Okay that's the introduction, let's get busy with the power of *17-Minute Sprints*.

If, like me, you have something you need to get done, but you find yourself losing focus or procrastinating then simply set a 17-minute timer.

'Alexa, give me a 17-minute reminder'

'Hey Siri! 17-minute countdown' — or Timer on Watch.

'Google, 17-minute timer'.

It doesn't matter which method you use, so long as you start your 17 minutes with **intent**.

17

For the next 17 minutes I will intently focus on the job in hand.

I'm doing this right now while writing this chapter. I know in 17 minutes I can write 450 words; and with a goal to write a minimum of 1,000 words a day then 3 x 17-minute sprints will get me over the line.

And that's the idea of the 17-minute sprint. Told you it's simple.

There are so many things you can use the 17-minute sprints for. Here are a few and how you could use them.

Flag/File/Delete
FFD.

Writing Emails + Sorting Emails

It can be painful to write emails. We think there may be time later in the day. Perhaps you can grab a few moments to respond using your phone during your journey home. Or when you get home? Before you know it, you're answering emails from the bedroom. And you wonder why your love life is suffering.

Set a 17-minute countdown and smash those emails. I think you'll be surprised at how many you can write, reply and send.

Sorting Emails

It isn't just writing the emails. Sometimes finding the time to read what has been sent to you can be challenging. So how about a 17-minute sprint where all you do is battle through your inbox and clear as many emails as possible? This isn't responding, it's just reading then FFD: flagging, filing or deleting.

Do this a few times and you'll find you regularly challenge yourself to use your 17-minute email sprint to beat your previous daily best.

Creating Reports

Some people (odd folk) love creating reports. Most people put this off, thinking that it's going to be boring and take ages. Why not create an amazingly detailed report in 17 minutes? Test this one. You'll be amazed.

Studying Data / *Doing Research*

Some people love studying data. If you think the report writers are odd, then check out this bunch. They also seem to be the people who have a greater understanding of the power of data. They make better, well-informed decisions, earn more and are ultimately more successful. Not so odd now!

Test out the technique. Set your 17-minute sprint timer and analyse industry and corporate data, feedback, and whatever else will improve your knowledge and level of awareness.

Calling Your Mum / *Sisters/Friends*

Of course, it doesn't have to be your mum, it's just that person who you know you should call but keep putting it off (yes, your sister). The reason I said mum is because my mum can talk for Britain. She can easily tell me the same story five times in the same week and not even know she's repeated it.[3]

---

[3] I realise that one day I will long to hear my mum tell me the same story five times over.

Based on that, I tell myself that I'll need plenty of time to call Mum. I'm busy now so I'd best call her later. But a 17-minute call is almost always long enough.

Who do you need to call? Maybe you just need to start the conversation with, 'I thought I'd give you a quick call.' You know you can make someone's day.

Tidying a Mess

At times, this is a physical mess: your desk, the shelves, a room or a drawer. Or it could be a virtual mess (see emails). How's your computer desktop? Do you have dozens of icons waiting to be filed or neat folders with everything that you need at your fingertips? And what about that cupboard under the stairs?

Cleaning a Room

A clean room feels better. Smells better. Looks better. It's more pleasant to enter. And you feel confident about bringing other people into your spick and span environment.

I know, you'd love to do it... if only you had a little more time. Maybe the weekend? 'When I have a few hours, I'll do a deep clean.' A month later, you can see the dust – and what's that funny smell?

Bring everything you need to hand, set a 17-minute timer and have a sprint. A cleaning sprint. Bathrooms will sparkle, bedrooms will feel fantastic (you'll sleep better) and that bacteria experiment you've been nurturing in your kitchen? It's gone.

Thinking

I often give my coaching clients the task of just sitting and thinking for 17 minutes. Not meditating – that's clearing the mind. This is thinking. It sounds easy, but actually doing nothing but thinking for 17 minutes can be challenging.

Let me make it very clear what this looks like. No TV. No reading. No notepad. No music. No food or drinks. No distractions. No phone (other than for the 17-minute reminder). No one else around you. Just you and your thoughts; for 17 minutes.

You may want to make sure you have a notepad available afterwards to capture all of the amazing thoughts you will have had in your 17-minute deep dive. See more on this in 17-Minute Deep Think on page 74.

Reading

17 minutes of really reading. Do a quick mental rehearsal: relax, close your eyes and see yourself reading the book and the information going into your mind. Feel yourself understanding the content, knowing how to apply it and remembering the key information. Then imagine you're increasing the speed of your reading. Open your eyes and you'll read faster. Practice increasing your speed further. Almost everyone can read 17% faster.

Writing

Earlier this year I launched a masterclass with 75 students who all wanted to write and publish a book. The excitement of signing up and joining the masterclass soon evolved into a realisation that the work had started, and the book had to be written. And, as every author knows, the only way to do this is one word at a time. Every book you have ever read has used the exact same formula. One – word – at – a – time.

Writer's block is real. Looking from keyboard to empty screen, to blank notebook, back to screen over and over is miserable. But it can be overcome by creating 17-minute writing sprints.

My challenge to these brilliant new authors is to write literary crap for 17 minutes. Yes, that's the challenge. 17 minutes of total crap. And only after they've written for 17 minutes can they can stop to review whatever they've written.

The results of the challenge are always the same. You cannot write crap for 17 minutes.

17

You cannot write crap for 17 minutes.

You may manage 15, but within those words there will be two minutes of something you're proud of. And maybe another five minutes of something that may need a little work, but can be improved upon. And okay, there will probably be 10 minutes of crap.

After that first 17-minute writing crap challenge, I encourage doubling down and having another 17-minute writing sprint. This time writing crap is harder. Most likely five to ten minutes of the writing will be good. There may still be some crap in there, but actually there's a lot more really good stuff. And importantly, you've started to find your groove.

Then the final 17-minute sprint of the hour. This is where you'll find out how good you really are. Word and sentence construction feel natural. The crap count will be down to a few minutes. Good and even excellent writing will start to be the norm now. And in one hour you have gone from writing mainly crap to writing several decent pages. You're an author.

The same goes for writing technical manuals, reports for the board, press releases, website content, and a dozen other writing tasks which could leave minds blank or be seen as a chore.

You'll find that once you've written for an hour, you can begin a 17-minute sprint entirely focused on…

Editing

Some people write, then forget to edit. A certain President of the United States has experienced this with his tweets. Journalists have written unchecked articles only to fall foul once the presses have rolled. Pubs have chalked-up signs (with comical effect). The editing process of any written work is essential. This may not take 17 minutes (it could be more or less) but it should be incorporated into every writing sprint.

Making Business Calls

The hardest part of making any call is picking up the phone. All salespeople either have, or have had, the fear of picking up the phone. You may be reading this thinking, thank goodness I'm not in sales. But you are. There are times when only a phone call will do.

And setting aside 17 minutes to make that call (or calls), to persuade, sell, encourage or reframe someone's thinking, could be the most lucrative 17 minutes of your day.

Journaling Your Day

Journaling is a habit used by many highly successful people. They know it's invaluable to capture your thoughts on paper at the end of each day. There's power in having a record of what you do, why you did it, what you were thinking and the impact it made.

If you need some encouragement to get started with journaling, could I suggest a 17-minute sprint at the end of each day for 17 days? As you progress with your journal, use part of your 17-minute sprint to reflect on what you did last week, last month or even last year. Recording your daily activity will become a big part of your life. It will chart your evolution and how your life is changing. You will gain strength from your journaling.

17

Journaling charts your evolution and how your life is changing. No excuses. Start today.

Playing with Your Kids

I was in two minds about whether to include this as a 17-minute sprint. Surely all parents can find more than 17 minutes to play with their kids? If that sounds like you then great. Just skip this 17-minute sprint and get on with being a brilliant parent. Or...

I know there were times when I convinced myself that I was spending time focused on entertaining my kids. Actually, I was amusing myself with (insert your favourite distraction here). Maybe you've experienced that too?

There's nothing wrong with saying 'Alexa, 17-minute countdown', before having a totally focused fun time and being completely in the moment. And when the beep says the 17 minutes are up, I bet you find you don't want to stop.

Preparing a Meal

You don't have time to cook from scratch, suggest so many adverts for ready meals. They want you to throw a pre-prepped meal into the microwave, fire it up for three minutes on high and wait for the 'ping'.

I get it, you're busy. But could you surprise yourself with what you could make in just 17 minutes if you focused on cooking a fantastic freshly prepared meal?

Just search The Google for '15-minute meals', do a bit of prep, then challenge yourself to complete a few simple 17-minute meal sprints this week. It gets easier, is healthier and tastes much better!

This list could go on, but I think you've got the idea.

If you should stop reading this book now, and only ever use 17-Minute Sprints, you will enjoy a massive change in your life. Make this a habit. As soon as you find yourself putting something off, pondering the size of the task or generally dilly-dallying, set the timer.

17 more things you can do in 17-Minute Sprints

1. Get ready to go out (bet you can)
2. Mini car valet
3. Send thank you cards
4. Ask your boss something
5. Manicure
6. Reduce your utility bill
7. Leave some intrusive WhatsApp groups
8. Set up a date
9. Listen to your favourite music
10. Clean your shoes
11. Sort out items for the charity shop
12. Have a nap
13. Fix something that's broken
14. Book an appointment (eyes, massage, car service, etc)
15. Check your computer's security
16. Descum the bathroom
17. Home admin

SPRINTS
in 17 words

In 17 minutes you cannot run a marathon

But you can run a mile

Do that

2. Why You Shouldn't Be in the Top 1%

It's often said that you should aim to be in the top 1%. I disagree. If you want to be successful, be in the top 17%. And aim for three areas of expertise.

Do this and you'll be in the top ½ percent in that area of specialist expertise in those three overlapping (often complementary) skills.

And being in the top 17% is accessible to everyone. Accessible because the main driver to being in the top 17% of anything is pure hard work.

17

As 83% of people aren't prepared to work as hard as you then you'll succeed.

Alhamdulillah, I am a good communicator!

Plus, if you make one of your three 17%s communication, it magnifies everything. I'd go so far as to say that being in the top 17% for communication is essential to every 17 student's success. Being able to communicate ideas, arguments, thoughts, etc amplifies everything you do. Basically, people who can communicate well will always do better than those who can't.

Here are a couple of scenarios where you could use the **17% x 3** method. Imagine this:

Why You Shouldn't Be in the Top 1%

You're an accountant – a top 17% employee in your company. That's good.

And you're an exceptional team player who adds value – again top 17%. That's fantastic.

You're a confident communicator. Happy to stand up and present on behalf of your department – top 17%. That's brilliant.

Any one of those top 17%s is good, but when you combine all three, that's when you get noticed.

The conversation about you goes like this:

'You know Julie from Accounts?'

'Of course. Good worker, she's on the People Panel too?'

'Yes, that's her. Did you see the information she presented at the Company Update on cost reduction? It was excellent. Loved how she turned £s into seconds. Really made us think. I'd like to give her more responsibility to explore this further.'

'Great, go for it.'

Notice how the conversation wasn't about departments and numbers. It was about an individual, her input and her presentation skills.

Or how about this. You're a coach. I know, the world suddenly appears to be full of coaches. So what makes you special?

You could become known as the world's most well-read coach on leadership. Big ask. Or you could start your own research project – which would take five years and cost you hundreds of thousands of pounds. Or you could become a celebrity coach and spend a fortune working with PR agencies, pitching for work with C-listers so you can attain the moniker 'celebrity life coach'. It's all very boring. And unachievable for most people – especially most coaches.

But what if you were in the top 17% of well-read coaches? I'm sure if you read just one book a week you would end up in that top 17% fairly quickly.

Now, what if you focused on being in the top 17% of well-connected coaches? Really using events, LinkedIn and other social media in an effective way. Helping to connect like-minded people and giving great value without asking for anything in return. Is that possible?

Then add brilliant customer service. Really bond with potential and current clients. Put massive deposits in their emotional bank accounts. You don't have to be a Ritz Carlton, just in the top 17%.

Finally why not add one more, the *communication magnifier*. And now you've gone from being 'just another coach', to a top 0.08% coach due to your unique offering.

It's worth taking a moment to consider what you want to be known for and where you are prepared to put in the work. There's little point in starting on this process unless you're prepared to do the graft as well as enjoy it.

My top three 17% areas to focus on are: Writing (I may just scrape into the top 17% here – you will be the judge of that). Coaching (again, I know people who are far more talented as coaches – my goal is to be in the top 17%). And speaking, where, having been described as one of the top three professional speakers in the world, I think I'm smashing the 17% with that one.

Notice I'm not in the top 17% for business, leadership, marketing, finances, and a dozen other areas where maybe you think I should be. I don't care. The day I chose what I wanted to focus on, and the fact that those three areas bring me so much pleasure, means I can work for long hours and never feel tired, bored or disillusioned.

17

What are your 3 top 17%s?

It doesn't need to be work. Choose areas in life that matter to you.

To be the top 1%, be the top 17% x 3:

Top 17% x Top 17% x Top 17% = Top 0.5%

Why You Shouldn't Be in the Top 1%

①

Here are 17 Top 17% ideas to get you started:

P 17% of Musallis in terms of Khushoo/Punctuality/Masjid

1 Could you be a top 17% parent?
   ↳ Use Azan Radio, Abida, TMP

2 What do the top 17% leaders do?

3 Everybody could be a top 17% employee. Actually, mathematically they couldn't, but that's alright because 90%+ won't read this book.

4 I bet you could be a top 17% friend or neighbour.

5 Analyst. The top 17% know how to draw out the important stuff.
   Eat less, ↑ Water ↑ Veg
   More walking

② 6 Top 17% money savvy.

7 You don't have to be an Olympian to be in the top 17% of fit and healthy people.

8 Considering how few people read, you're probably already in the top 17% of readers. But could you give yourself a boost?

9 Technology. Do you understand the fundamentals of the tech that powers your life or business?

10 Negotiation. Not sure about this one? Well you can take it or leave it.

11 Son/daughter. Your parents will like this.

12 Futurist. Learn more about what's happening in the future, be an opportunist and apply that thinking now.

13 Customer. Flip it: as well as being a top 17% supplier be a top customer.

14 Human. Watch the news (once) and look at most of the people featured. Do the opposite. Be in the top 17%.

15 Emotional intelligence. This should be a must.

16 Creative. Open your mind, be diverse, be imaginative.

17 Specialist. What specialism could you focus on to be in the 17%?

③ Top 17% of husbands.
   Itol time daily.
   Weekly date.
   ↳ Following on from this, Top 17% of parents.

17 words on being in the top 17%

The best didn't get there by accident

It's almost always down to skill meets opportunity meets graft

3. 17 Ways to Be Brilliant at Work

Often this type of book is tailored towards entrepreneurs and business owners. This is crazy, as the vast majority of people aren't entrepreneurs or business owners. But that doesn't stop you from being an *intrapreneur*: someone who has an entrepreneurial mindset and works *within* an organisation.

Because you're reading this book, I'm guessing that you're the type of person who wants to do well, to make a difference and (I'm guessing) you're quite ambitious. And why not be?

This is one of those easy-to-read, quick-to-finish, full of intent *but* challenging to put in place, chapters. Therefore, could I suggest you put six or seven ideas in place (the ones you know you could be better at), and make them stick? The same applies to business owners too.

As with any list like this, there will be things you already do. Revel in the glory of this moment. Now challenge yourself to focus on the ones you don't do.

1. Arrive Early

It still surprises me the number of times people are supposed to start work at 9am and arrive at work at... 9. Even though you may stay late, it won't be noticed nearly as much as if you arrive early. Staying late can be associated with not getting your work done. Whereas arriving early is associated with the intention to get your work done.

2. Have a Clean, Clear Desk/Workspace

Removing distractions from your desk creates an instant good impression and makes it easier for you to work. Too obvious? I would also have a small tin of furniture polish and a dust cloth in your drawer. On Friday night, before you leave, clear your desk and give it a quick polish.

If you're reading this and considering that this is the job of the office cleaner, then I think you might have just missed the point.

3. Do the Job You Wish to Be Promoted to - Before You're Promoted

'If I was promoted, I would definitely do a better job than them,' he whined. How about doing a better job than them *before* you're promoted? Those who are promoted fastest are normally doing the job they were promoted to long before they received the official recognition.

This is a mindset that some people just can't get their heads around. They want to receive first, then give. Being brilliant at work is giving first and then receiving.

4. Look Good and Smile

Have you noticed some people bring a permanent frown to work? They always look upset about something. If you ask if they're okay, they invariably say yes. Resist the temptation to say, 'Well tell your face!' A pleasant smile will make your colleagues, customers and bosses more likely to like you.

And take a moment to consider your appearance. Take pride in how you look, check your breath, spend an extra 10 seconds in front of the mirror and tell yourself you're looking good.

17

The sides of your mouth should be moving in the same direction as you'd like your salary to be headed.

5. Volunteer

Don't wait to be asked. Volunteer to take on a task or responsibility. The idea of keeping your head down doesn't work for someone who wants to be on Team 17. Bosses know how brilliant it is to have someone in a team who volunteers rather than needs to be persuaded to do something. Make that person you. When promotions, pay rises and progressions are available, the volunteers will always be at the top of any list.

6. Avoid Gossip

Work is a hotbed for gossip. Avoid it if you can. If you can't, learn how to sidestep. I remember a wonderful colleague who, whenever she was presented with a morsel of gossip, simply said 'Is that so?' and then moved the conversation on. If your idea of strictest confidence is only telling other people one at a time, maybe it's time to avoid the gossip.

7. Positively Impact the Environment

Everyone can make a difference to our planet at work; by reducing your carbon footprint, protecting the environment and saving precious resources. One of my favourite TED Talk videos is by Joe Smith. It's called 'How to use a paper towel'. In just 4 minutes he beautifully demonstrates how to use only one of a selection of paper towels to completely dry your hands.

Whether it's a car share, using company resources carefully, recycling, turning the lights off or any of the hundreds of things we know we should do (but don't always do), please do them.

8. Live Your Company Values

Does your organisation have a set of company values? Are they simply a list of ideals or something real that everyone lives by? When you have a difficult decision to make, your first stop should always be your company values. Does doing X take you closer to or move you further away from living the company values? If it takes you closer to – do it. Further away – don't. I appreciate it's not always as black and white as this, but it's a great place to start.

9. Know Your Industry

Taking the time to really understand your industry/sector will pay huge dividends. Is there a trade body? Are people writing articles? Is there a magazine or website for your sector? Who's saying what? Who are the influencers? Are you connected with them through, for example, LinkedIn?

Industry knowledge is accessible to everyone and yet only a handful of people bother to take the time to dig deep and find out what's happening outside of their organisation.

10. Paradigm Shift with Your Boss

Some people have a love/could like more[4] relationship with their boss. One minute they are a real piece of work with no idea what you're having to deal with. The next, an incredible supportive individual who you couldn't manage without. Guess what? Your boss is having the same battle too. Even if they're the big boss, they're still human. Which means they'll make mistakes, misjudge certain situations and at times p*** you and others off. By taking a moment to experience a paradigm shift you'll start to see things from their perspective. It doesn't mean you have to like what they do, it just makes it easier to understand and accept.

11. Know the Numbers   *Top 20, Look at Springboard.*

All organisations rely on getting the numbers right. It's not just the job of Finance to know the numbers, it's the responsibility of everyone. If you know how your organisation creates income, the associated running costs, acceptable margins, where there's waste and what to do about it, you'll be in the top 17%.

When you take an interest in the numbers, the statistics, and are able to compare year on year (or quarter on quarter/week on week) that's a powerful place to be. Next, have a goal to make a positive difference to those numbers.

12. Put the Customer First - Always

This should be a no-brainer, yet I'm staggered by the number of companies, and their employees, who don't understand the importance of the customer. All organisations have customers, internal and external, and everything you do should benefit them.

---

[4] That's what positive people say instead of 'hate'.

Notice I'm not saying *the customer is always right*, they're not. And notice I'm not saying *do whatever it takes to keep a customer* – some customers you're better off without. What I am saying is think customer first.

13. Be Clear in Your Communications

When you reach chapter 5, which is all about communication, make sure you're poised with pen in hand. Apply the tools and techniques I've shared there in all of your communications. Written, telephone, one to one, small and large groups… anywhere that you need to communicate, do it well. It's the magnifier.

14. Avoid Work Politics

Work politics are sure to cause more problems than they fix in the long run. You can't win. Because if you're the one playing office politics and you do win, it still means somebody had to lose. And thinking win/lose is never going to be good in the long term. I promise you – the fact that somebody appears to have 'got away with it' in the past doesn't give you a pass to do the same. Avoid.

15. Be a Brilliant Learner

Sign up for every course, read the books, ask for coaching, find a mentor, learn from top performers, keep good records and apply what you learn.

The top learners are the top earners.

17

16. Build Relationships with Stakeholders

These people can be colleagues, directors, suppliers. In fact, anyone who has an impact on your work and that of your organisation. Often, you'll find people frantically trying to build relationships with their stakeholders **at the time** they need them. It's too late. It usually means your emotional bank account is already overdrawn. Smart people will have built the relationships in advance and have lots of deposits in their stakeholders' emotional bank accounts.

17. Do Your Job

This seems ridiculously obvious and yet, from working with thousands of organisations and coaching hundreds of leaders, I've seen this is a massive frustration. Even though staff are being paid to do a job, at times they just don't deliver. They're nice people, great to be around, say 'yes' at all the right times. They just don't deliver.

You could spend a lot of time and energy working on the first 16 points on this list and they won't make much difference if you're not doing this one. Do your job – do it brilliantly.

Hard work beats talent. By focusing and delivering on this list of 17 things, I promise you will be noticed, remembered and referred.

17 jobs I've had

1 Paper boy
2 Consultant
3 Slater and tiler
4 Community fundraiser
5 Youth worker
6 Magician
7 Charity director
8 Project manager
9 Internet entrepreneur
10 Author
11 Coach
12 Partner in a training company
13 Marketing manager
14 Keyboard player
15 Company director
16 Professional speaker
17 Balloonologist

WORK
in 17 words

You spend a third of your life and half your waking hours at work

So love it

4. 17% More or Less

A simple chapter on the power of just 17% more or less and the extraordinary impact it can have:

(1)

17% More Sleep
Aim to sleep straight after Isha Salah (Floss + brush before)

Being sleep deprived can have a massive impact on multiple areas of your life. If you're only getting six hours and 50 minutes out of your recommended eight hours sleep (yes, you do need more sleep) that's a sleep deficit of 426 hours in a year. That's 17 whole 24-hour days! Increase your sleep by 17% and pay off that sleep debt.

(2)

17% Less Calories
Large Glass of Water before each meal + More Salad.

There's a whole bunch of science (I'm not going to go into it here) that demonstrates by creating a slight calorie deficit you will live longer, feel healthier and have numerous other health benefits. If you're normally eating 2,000 calories a day test how you feel on 1,700.

(6)

17% More Reading Speed
— Practice Speed Reading Drills

If the average person reads at 250 words a minute, by increasing your reading speed by 17% you could devour an extra 2,550 words an hour. That means you could read this book faster and add a couple of 17-minute sprints to apply the ideas.

17% Less Screen Time
Your phone is probably measuring it and will give you a weekly update of how much screen time you have being inflicting on your retinas. Could you cut down by 17%? → *Cut down on News, emails*

17% More Play Time

If you're lucky enough to have children who still want to spend time with you, then give them 17% more. Every extra minute spent now will pay off for the rest of your – and their – lives. If you have a hobby could you spend 17% more time on it? If you're lucky enough to have a partner, you could have 17% more play time too...

17% More Time on Your Meal *Chew each morsel 17 times!*

I love my food but at times can be a food hoover. Spending 17% longer really enjoying every mouthful, taking in all the tastes and textures, will not only make the meal more enjoyable, it will help you to digest it too. Your colon doesn't have teeth.

17% More Focus on Your Partner

This is a tough one, especially as my brilliant wife, Christine, is editing this book and has barely seen me for the last few weeks. 17% more focus. Really. It's not a should, it's a must. See 17% more play time.

17% More Time on a Journey

We humans always seem to be in a hurry to get somewhere. How about taking it easy, setting off a bit earlier and taking 17% longer to get there? You'll be safer and arrive feeling fresher.

17% Saving on Your Monthly Spend

I was going to include a whole chapter on ways to save 17%, but there are some amazing websites that will show you how to do this much better than me. I'd focus on scheduling some time (a few 17-minute sprints will do it) to look at your outgoings, cutting out or reducing bad spending habits, and making considered decisions on where you will be happy to hand over your hard-earned cash.

17% More Physical Activity *More fast walks daily, even if 5 mins at a time.*

Could you spend 17% more time on your physical activity? That's not much, and the benefits could be huge. If you normally do a 30-minute workout, 17% more is just 5 minutes.

17% Less TV

yes!

What if you stopped watching the news? Seriously, how many times do you need to see it? And I'm constantly amazed at how many people think they haven't got the time to improve the quality of their lives, but will happily binge-watch a Netflix series for two or three hours a day. Reduce that by 17% and there's at least two hours a week to spend doing something amazing.

If I had 17% more 'me time' I'd use it just to hang out. Here's where.

17 places to hang out

5 hrs away!

1. The beach, Cresswell — *100K up. Camber Sands was also beautiful*
2. The Port, Ibiza Town
3. The whole Lake District *+ Peak District, Norfolk, Suffolk*
4. King's Cross Station, London
5. Central Park, New York
6. Quayside, Newcastle upon Tyne
7. Airport arrivals
8. A music festival
9. The Squares in Malmö, Sweden
10. Soho, London
11. The Bondi Icebergs Club (The Bergs), Bondi
12. Barcelona, all of it
13. Aguas Blancas, Ibiza
14. Fenwick Food Hall, Newcastle
15. Boat Quay, Singapore
16. Venice Beach, Los Angeles
17. Home

17 words on
MORE OR LESS

Would it matter if, on this occasion, a 17 words page wasn't exactly 17 words?

More or less

17 in Communication: The Magnifier

How long should a speech, presentation or video last? My answer is usually, 'Never too long. Only too boring.'

But it transpires that there *is* a perfect length of time for an outstanding, non-boring presentation. And I bet you can guess how long it is... Yes, around 17 minutes.

Martin Luther King's historic 'I have a dream' – 17 minutes.

Steve Jobs launching the iPhone – 4 x 17 minutes. An initial 17-minute overview, then 17 mins on each of the main features.

Simon Sinek, 'Start with Why' – 17 minutes.

Coincidence? I don't think so. TED Talks (should) last for a maximum of 18 minutes. The majority are just short – 17.

17

If you can't say what you need to say in 17 minutes, then maybe it needs an edit.

This is one of the meatiest chapters in this book. As you know from earlier chapters, I consider great communication to be the magnifier of everything you do. So, it's worth taking time to really delve in and PRACTICE what you learn here.

To be a brilliant communicator you don't have to be naturally brilliant at communication. Just follow the 17 rules of communication

THEN you can become a brilliant communicator.

And as video (web comms) becomes an even more popular medium for making presentations, building personal brand, holding meetings and going 'live' then what used to be a required skill for the few is now an essential asset for the many.

We teach a powerful and fun workshop called *How to Be a Super Speaker* for participants at every level of communicating ability. We've taught it to thousands for over 20 years so I am convinced *anyone* can become a significantly better communicator by following these rules, tips, tools and tricks.

Don't Try Too Hard

It's weird but when some people need to make a presentation, they are impelled into some strange sort of pseudo-Hollywood song and dance routine. They think they should be Preston's answer to Tony Robbins when all they're doing is delivering the quarterly profit and loss update.

I've seen chief executives at the annual conference transform into corporate evangelical preachers just to welcome staff back after lunch. You can feel the audience cringing. For the best example, search 'Steve Ballmer Runs Around Like a Maniac on Stage'. This is the chief executive of Microsoft arriving on stage for a company update. He actually injures himself getting onto the platform and is so worn out after his run around he can hardly speak.

I'm sure Steve has 17 billion reasons why he couldn't care less. However, my advice is, just be +1 from where your audience are. If they are already energetic and upbeat, then you should also be energetic and upbeat... +1 (but not using Steve B metrics).

If your audience is neutral, don't start to present at their level – be +1. Lift them a little. And if your audience are a bunch of moany-faced, miserable, energy-sapping, neg-heads... don't join them. But also, please don't try to bring them up to highly motivated and enthused all in one go – just use +1. When you get them up to your level, and only if there's time, take them to the next level. +1 again.

self - Just Your Better Self

I've hea.. people offer varying advice pre-presentation, especially 'Just be yourself'. This is poor advice, as most people's selves aren't great communicators. So, could I suggest you be yourself – just a better version of yourself? Look at your communication style. Be honest. Identify and develop your authentically strong communication traits, remove the bad habits that hold you back and temper the bits in the middle.

Let's start by removing the bad habits.

As a professional speaker, I've been in the audience for literally thousands of events, and in that time I have seen tens of thousands of people speak. Never doubt the power of words. Here are several examples to use if you're intent on *losing* your audience faster than you can say 'What time's the coffee break?' Brace yourself: you may have said or done one or two of these in the past.

17

> **Don't be yourself. Be a better version of yourself.**

1. This is the boring bit

I know it can be endearing to be self-deprecating. But really, when can pre-framing your presentation with 'this is going to be boring' ever be helpful?

2. I know you can't read this...

This is a symptom of using PowerPoint as a crutch rather than a support tool. If you have that awful realisation that your presentation can't be seen, just talk through it anyway AND DON'T POINT IT OUT. Read the advice on PowerPoint in number 5.

3. Does that make sense?

During a presentation, asking 'Does that make sense?' says more about the presenter then the audience. It's one of those phrases that comes up when the presenter lacks confidence in their message rather than as a genuine check to see if your audience are still with you. Change it for a positive: 'All good?'

4. Using any kind of acronym

TLAs are liberally thrown around every organisation. Never a problem if you know what they mean, but embarrassing if you don't. Would you be brave enough to put your hand up and ask what something meant if everyone else was nodding? No. And neither would your audience. So be the presenter who always gives a full description and removes the Three-Letter Acronyms.

5. Relying on PowerPoint

PowerPoint is a wonderful tool, but avoid DBPP – Death By PowerPoint (sorry, four-letter acronym snuck in there!). You can either put your whole presentation on your slides and have the audience read them (so you don't need to speak) or present to your audience so that they listen.

But don't do both.

Use this as a rule of thumb: no more than 10 words on each slide – maximum. There may be the odd exception, such as quoting individuals or ensuring an exact phrase or sentence is used. In most cases, just use fewer words.

PowerPoint is a prop. Your audience aren't listening to you while they attempt to read small cluttered text or decipher complicated graphs.

Now let's take a look at some of the things which should feature in every presentation. And, of course, there are 17.

at Start

Vita.., important for any communication. Ask The Google 'how much time do you have to grab an audience's attention?' It suggests between five minutes and seven seconds. I think you have about a minute to get your audience engaged and thinking. That's why I like starting by asking questions. Here are some great openers.

Have you ever wondered…?

Wouldn't it be great if we…?

Why is it that every time…?

Am I the only person who…?

When you ask a question (like the ones above), you create what's known as an 'open loop'. Your audience begin to answer the question for themselves, but they are naturally interested in what you think, as you posed the question.

Never answer the question at the beginning of your presentation. That's called 'closing the loop' which, wherever possible, happens towards the end of your presentation.

Have a think about your opening question. Here are a few that others have used which can help to get you started:

Have you ever wondered… why four in five businesses fail in the first few years and what the one that survives does differently?

Wouldn't it be great if we… didn't need to hold meetings ever again?

Why is it that every time… I need loose change, I can't find any? And yet when I don't need any I have pockets full?

Am I the only person who… believes we could increase our effectiveness and at the same time reduce our costs?

2. Prepare, Prepare, Prepare

When you arrive at a restaurant at 7pm for dinner, you know that the chefs didn't rock up just before you at 6.55. All good restaurants spend hours preparing the food. The final part of the process is the few minutes before it arrives at your table. Your presentation should be the same.

The number one reason why most people delivering a presentation (or any communication) fail to get their message across, bore their audience – or both – is that they didn't prepare.

I think you should be looking for a minimum ratio of 10:1 preparation time to presenting. If you have to do a 15-minute presentation – work on it for at least 2½ hours. That may seem excessive, but if it's important and you really want to make an impact, this will be some of the best time you ever invest.

I plan everything, even the off-the-cuff stuff. If I use it, great. If I don't, fine. It's there for the next time. I love this quote from Mark Twain:[5]

17

'I would sometimes spend months planning how to be spontaneous' – Mark Twain

3. Breathe

I've stood backstage many times and watched presenters overcome with nerves at the prospect of walking out in front of their audience. I've observed (normally calm) people in a meeting await their slot on the agenda and I've watched their physiology negatively change as it gets closer.

And much of it is down to... breathing.

I'd suggest before any presentation – and this includes important phone calls, updates, speaking up in a meeting, anywhere you need to use your voice – that you take a few breaths using the 3-4-5 method. You breathe in for three seconds, hold the breath for four seconds then breathe out for five. Do it now. Three times.

If you're reading this sentence and you haven't done this simple breathing exercise, then please stop reading and do it now.

---

[5] Mark Twain must have spent hours writing quotes. Search for Mark Twain quote and add almost any subject and you'll find something.

id the exercise (and I'm trusting you here) then you should
ed how calm you are feeling. Imagine, the next time you're
sent, instead of feeling nervous, just breathe… 3-4-5. Ahhhhh.

4. Mentally Rehearse

You are probably already mentally rehearsing your presentation many times over before you deliver it. And you're probably mentally rehearsing the wrong thing.

I've had the nightmares too. The ones where you walk on stage and realise you're in your underpants. Or the one where you try to speak, but nothing comes out. Or you can't even park because you're driving the car from the back seat and your feet won't reach the pedals. Then there are the stories you tell yourself. I'm going to be rubbish. They won't listen. Look at that audience, they won't like me.

You need to create a new outcome and you can do this by mentally rehearsing. The right things.

I used to encourage people only to mentally rehearse positive outcomes. Now I think it's important to mentally rehearse for every eventuality – but always with a final positive outcome. For example, if you have to present to a group of colleagues and you know a couple of them may not give you their full attention, (or might even be disruptive), mentally rehearse that situation. Then – and this is key – see yourself overcoming that challenge and delivering brilliantly. They won't be remembered for their giggles, but you will be remembered for your amazing presentation.

Here are a few things you can mentally rehearse:

Your opening

Your closing

Potential questions

Using your technology. Practice where something might go wrong and how you would deal with it

Complicated information

The reactions of the people who you're presenting to – a standing ovation?

Feeling relaxed and comfortable. See this from the audience view and from your view

Being thanked after the presentation for doing such a great job

5. Timing - Get There Early

Often, timing means comic timing or timing for dramatic effect. Although that's important, none of this matters if you're not there on time.

> **17**
>
> **Even if you are presenting in the same building – be there early.**

Don't be the person desperately trying to set up PowerPoint while their busy colleagues wait around, looking at their watches. It's unprofessional and puts you under too much pressure.

And if you're presenting on a big stage, make sure you're there well before the audience. Make friends with the production team, check everything works, *then* have a coffee.

6. Have a Start, Middle and End

You've watched the news and you know the format. It's the same every time, worldwide. 'Here are the headlines' followed by the news. Then, 'Here's a final look at the headlines.' Basically, it's telling the audience what they *will* learn, telling them something and finally reminding them what they *have* learned.

Although this is predictable (I would rather start with a question), knowing that your presentation has a very clear start, a bit in the middle (your stuff) and a very clear end will help you to communicate brilliantly.

Once you're clear, and you're happy with your start, practice it so many times that you could do it in your sleep. You probably will.

.e a Mistake... Get Over It

reframe this. *When* you make a mistake get over it. I do

and speaking is my job. As soon as you apologise – 'Oh,

ed a bit', 'That didn't work', 'That should have been this' or 'that', ... oops that didn't happen in rehearsal...' – you've drawn the focus of your audience to what went wrong.

Nobody knows that you've missed something unless you tell them. You can seriously mess up the numbers and you'll be amazed at how few people would spot it.

I once watched Dennis Turner, at that time the chief economist for HSBC, present to a group of business owners for 15 minutes before he realised he was using the wrong slide deck. He'd done the presentation so many times he didn't need to look at the slides. He spoke with such confidence nobody realised. When he did spot his error, (and he didn't mention it) he simply stopped his presentation, opened the right PowerPoint and started from where he'd left off.

8. Make Sure It's About Your Audience

That means it's not about you. Whenever anyone starts a presentation with, 'Let me tell you a little bit about me', a fairy dies. And you don't want a reputation as a fairy killer. Seriously, what really dies is your chance to make your point. Because, let me be ruthlessly honest here: no – one – cares – about – you.

If your audience hasn't found something that benefits them in the first two minutes of your communication, then you can forget the next 15. They will.

9. Less Is More

Understand that less really is more and time doesn't exist when you're presenting.

If you're planning a 17-minute presentation, I would suggest that when you practice it lasts for no more than 14 minutes. When you come to deliver the presentation, it will last for the full 17. There's a strange phenomenon that *all* presentations last for 17% more time than you practiced. If you have to speak for ten minutes make sure your practice is around eight. If you have to do an hour, prepare 50 minutes – maximum.

> **17**
>
> What happens if a miracle should occur and you finish early? Don't worry, your audience will love you even more.

10. Use the Power of Three

You're probably wondering why I'm not saying use the power of 17? Because 'three' really is a magic number. Especially in communication:

Friends, Romans, Countrymen

Education, Education, Education

Inform, Educate, Entertain

What are three ways you can use the power of three in your next three presentations?

11. Silence Is Golden

You don't have to fill all of your time with words. I've been doing a lot of live presentations on LinkedIn and Facebook lately and I've realised that you don't have to fill every moment with words. In fact, on those platforms, it's best if you don't talk all the time.

If you're doing a presentation in front of people you can see, you can read them quite easily and know... for how long... it's okay to pause. At the right time, a powerful pause can be used for incredible dramatic effect.

12. (If Possible) Get Eye Contact

I know it isn't always feasible to get eye contact (especially in this exciting new online broadcasting world) but if you can, do.

If you're live in a room, ensure you've looked at every single person

ce. Even if there's 1,000 people, look in the general area of
of the crowd and talk to them, directly, for 30 seconds or more.
re presenting online, look straight into the lens of your
camera. If you're looking at your own image on your iPad or phone then
your audience isn't seeing you, they're seeing a person who's looking
slightly off to one side. You've seen that before and know how
disconcerting it can be.

Camera Presenting Tip: When I do a presentation directly to my
phone or iPad, I stick a small piece of 'white tack' as close to the lens
as possible. Then, when I speak, I direct my presentation to the white
tack. As far as the audience is concerned, I'm looking straight at them.

13. Tell a Story

For thousands of years we have communicated by telling stories.

However, crafting a good story can be challenging. If it's a story
about something that has happened to you, then don't simply rely on
retelling it. Write it down, revise it as if you were a ruthless editor who
had to remove a third of the words so that it was punchy enough to
print in a magazine. If you are in any doubt that part of the story is
boring, or unnecessary, then I'll help you to remove that doubt. It is.

17

1 good story is worth 100 dull facts.

14. Practice Out Loud

Most people practice their presentation sitting at a desk. They say their
words in their heads, while tapping through slides on a keyboard. This
is a completely fake environment and it's unlikely you would ever
present like this.

I'll repeat, they practice by saying the words *in their heads*.

You must practice out loud. It's the only way to genuinely be able to time your presentation, know where you might trip up and discover whether your presentation really works. It will feel false and clunky at first, but the more often you practice by saying the words out loud, the easier it becomes.

This method of rehearsal will pay back 17-fold for every slightly embarrassing moment you experience practicing out loud.

15. Use Analogies and Metaphors

This is particularly useful when you have something complicated to explain. By saying 'It's like...', then adding a wonderful explanation that everyone understands and can connect with, is one of the most important tools in a great communicator's toolbox.

Relating a situation to sport, popular culture, household appliances, making a journey, and hundreds of other knowns, will help you to get your point across.

I could give you an explanation of how an electrical resistor works by quoting from Wikipedia.

A resistor is a passive two-terminal electrical component that implements electrical resistance as a circuit element. In electronic circuits, resistors are used to adjust signal levels, to divide voltages, bias active elements, and terminate transmission lines, among other uses.

Resistors are common elements of electrical networks and electronic circuits and are ubiquitous in electronic equipment. Practical resistors as discrete components can be composed of various compounds and forms. Resistors are also implemented within integrated circuits.

The electrical function of a resistor is specified by its resistance: common commercial resistors are manufactured over a range of more than nine orders of magnitude. The nominal value of the resistance falls within the manufacturing tolerance, indicated on the component.

Or say, 'You know when you squeeze a hose pipe to reduce the amount of water that comes through? That's what a resistor does with electricity.'

Your Stuff

...t started teaching personal development, I remember getting very excited about learning a new tool and immediately wanting to teach it. This worked well... to a point. When I started working with very bright people who asked really intricate questions, I began to struggle. Thankfully, Professor John MacBeath came into my life as a mentor, and he taught me a very simple rule. Only teach the tip of the iceberg. John encouraged me to study the science, find out why these theories worked, strive to know more than my audience. But never attempt to teach all of it.

Looking back and without anything other than a gut feel, I was probably teaching 80% of what I knew. Working with John, reading, attending events and learning from others flipped this and I ended up teaching 20%.[6] Knowing your stuff gives you confidence.

17

Learn the whole iceberg. Only teach the tip.

17. Have a Big Finish

When you're presenting and you want people to leave with a specific thought or call to action, don't end your presentation with 'Does anybody have any questions?' You won't receive questions, which equals flat finish, or you'll get questions that you can't answer or someone will throw you a complete curveball.

If you're going to take questions, could I suggest you say, 'Before I end, I'm going to take this opportunity to answer any questions you may have.' Then take the questions. Keep in mind how long your closing takes. You'll know this, because you will have practiced out

---

[6] The more I've thought about this the more I realise the lower the what-you-know to what-you-share ratio goes, the more confident you feel. Now one of my favourite parts of a presentation is questions. I used to dread it.

loud and be absolutely certain that your big finish is going to take one minute and eight seconds. Close the questions and say 'My final thoughts…' and wow them with your amazing close.

17 of my favourite audiobooks/programmes by some brilliant communicators

1   *Believe Me* – Eddie Izzard

2   Anything by Bill Bryson but let's go with *At Home*

3   *Think and Grow Rich* – The original one with audios of Napoleon Hill

4   *Why We Sleep* – Matthew Walker

5   *The Power of Now* – Eckhart Tolle

6   *Loving What Is* – Byron Katie

7   ALL the Harry Potters – JK Rowling and read by Stephen Fry

8   *Till The Cows Come Home* – Sara Cox

9   *The 4 Pillar Plan* – Dr Rangan Chatterjee

10 *Little Me* – Matt Lucas

11 *The eMyth Revisited* – Michael Gerber

12 *Becoming Johnny Vegas* – Johnny Vegas

13 *The Willpower Instinct* – Kerry McGonigal

14 *I, Partridge: We need to talk about Alan* – Steve Coogan/Alan Partridge

15 *Long Walk to Freedom* – Nelson Mandela

16 *The Sales Bible* – Jeffrey Gitomer

17 *Tribes* – Seth Godin

COMMUNICATION
in 17 words

Learning to be a great communicator can help hide your weaknesses and will magnify your best bits

6. Forced Rhubarb

It may be a timely moment in 17 to consider your readiness for greatness. Yes, greatness. And to do this let's talk rhubarb.

Yorkshire forced rhubarb is an out-of-season rhubarb. It is first grown outside for a period of two years so that exposure to frost toughens its roots. After the initial frost exposure, the rhubarb is transferred to 'forcing sheds'. Once in the darkened sheds, heat is applied, causing the rhubarb to grow quickly.

It searches for light.

To maintain the tenderness of the shoots, the rhubarb is harvested by candlelight. If the crowns (the chunky bit at the base) are exposed to too much light they will cease to grow. Photosynthesis will occur and the rhubarb will taste bitter.

The sticks are harvested by hand to prevent other crowns rotting from botrytis. After harvesting, the crowns are composted. This helps to ensure a more sustainable production.

This process produces rhubarb that is sweeter and more delicately flavoured. It also has an especially vivid red colour.

'Forced' is the word that stands out. By forcing the rhubarb to stretch, they are able to harvest the sweetest crop.

BUT... And this is the easy part to miss...

The forced rhubarb has had two years of preparation; becoming hardy, strong and resilient first. Forcing rhubarb, someone close or even yourself to grow without controlled exposure to the elements won't give you the sweet results.

You're more likely to have a bitter end.

It could be two weeks, two months or two years from start to finish. But don't miss some exposure to the frost first.

> **17**

> **Prepare first. Weather the storms. Then go for growth.**

I first ate forced rhubarb at one of these wonderful places. Any idea which one?

17 Amazing places to eat[7]

1 Hjem – Wall, Northumberland
2 Union Square Café – New York
3 The Rat Inn – Anick, Hexham
4 L'Enclume – Cartmel
5 Café 21 – Newcastle
6 Lake Road Kitchen – Ambleside, Cumbria
7 Kiku, London
8 Kingfisher – Port de Sóller, Mallorca
9 La Taberna de la Niña del Pisto, Marbella
10 Beach House – Elviria
11 Agroturismo Terra e Sapori – Castellammare Di Stabia (Pompie), Italy
12 All'Antico Vinaio, Florence
13 Dinner by Heston, London
14 Restaurant Le Musée, Lyon
15 Juan y Andrea – Formentera, Balearic Islands
16 Fire & Dough (mobile pizza company)
17 My kitchen – best food on the planet

---

[7] I'm aware several are in the North East of England. And some may have closed or changed by the time you read this.

17 words on STRETCHING YOURSELF AND YOUR ABILITY

You can't do splits after ten minutes stretching

You won't change the world after ten days trying

7. Your Massive Action Project

Everyone needs a Massive Action Project from time to time. After all, massive action = massive results. Every – single – time. A Massive Action Project is something that requires huge amounts of effort and energy. It's not for everyone – but then again, not everyone wants massive results.

You can set any length of time, but may I suggest 17 days?

I think you will be astounded at what you can get done in 17 days. And, if you need longer, break it down into 17-day chunks.

We've used the 90 days of Massive Action[8] format with clients for quite some time. It's an ideal time frame to completely redesign and improve the way things run. Often how the whole organisation runs. I've used 90 days to coach Premiership footballers from the reserve bench to a place on the England team. I've worked with entrepreneurs who have invented, developed, created, produced, marketed and sold a new product in 90 days.

In my experience, for most coaching clients the vast majority of the change takes place in the first couple of weeks. Or for the sake of this book, the first 17 days. 17 days is long enough to: change a mindset, transform a process, reorder, find another way, implement new ways of working. In the remaining 73 days you test and tweak everything you created in the first 17.

Here are a few guidelines to making your Massive Action Project enjoyable and effective.

---

[8] Of all the work we do, teaching Massive Action Projects is one of the most rewarding. The buzz of discovering something that was stuck or might have taken months can be sorted in weeks (or often days) is amazing.

Start with a Definite, Clear Purpose

It's difficult to create a Massive Action Project based on something woolly like:

We need to be better

We have to increase sales

I want to be fitter

I need to think about my career

A definite clear purpose would be:

We will launch a new product that will give us market advantage

I will increase my personal sales by 10%

I will lose 10 pounds and be able to run 5K

I will have applied for a job in a field that I love and be mentally ready and prepared for the selection process

Both lists are outcome based, but which option inspires you to take action?

Schedule Time

Carefully plan the time you need to work on your Massive Action Project. If you're already maxed it's unlikely that you're going to find the time needed to even get started. Look ahead in your diary and carve out the time you need to take the necessary action.

This could mean working outside of your normal hours. Schedule this time in too.

17

What gets scheduled gets done.

Resources

...o hand before you start your Massive Action Project. ...ointing to get off to a great start, only to realise you have to wait three days for a particular resource to become available to you.

For example, Day 1 – prep room and strip old wallpaper. Days 2–16... wait for new wallpaper which you didn't realise would be on back order for close to two weeks. Oh, and live with the disorder you've created. This is not the best way to start your Decorate the Lounge Massive Action Project.

Keep Good Records

Have you moved forward every day with your project? If not, why not? Massive Action Projects need to be reviewed every single day. Unless progress is made daily, the energy and enthusiasm fizzles out.

Remember, this is not a new way of working. This is a one-off project which demands results. When it's complete, you'll review your progress and consider what you will do differently next time.

Be Demanding

A 17-day Massive Action Project may not be the best time to win friends and influence people. It may be a perfect time to let those close to you know what you are planning so that they're aware from the outset.

I'm not suggesting you go all Elton John, tantrums and tiaras. But your taking Massive Action can mean a few withdrawals from the emotional bank accounts of those around you.

What will your first 17-day Massive Action Project – MAP – look like? Business? Personal? Health? Home? What have you been putting off that with 17 days of Massive Action you could kick-start or complete?

Make your first MAP a masterpiece.

This book was written using the 17 Days of Massive Act formula. Here's how I did it:

I started this project by launching a private Facebook Group called 17. I did this for three reasons:

1 Facebook Groups are fun. They're a great way to share ideas and to create an environment where people can meet for discussion. I've launched several Facebook Groups and have a formula to ensure that they are a beacon of positivity for the members.

2 I knew I wanted to write a book and I was pretty sure it was going to be 17. By starting the group, I had 375 supporters (and critics) sharing their thoughts and ideas.

3 By announcing that 17 would be a pop-up group and that it would only exist for 17 days, I created a deadline.

My definite and clear purpose was that I would write a new book, sell enough copies to make it viable and have a clear pathway for its publication and distribution.

The timescale was always going to be a challenge. I know I can write quickly: Christine and I wrote our first book *How to Be Brilliant* in just four days. However, my last book, *The Edge: how the best get better*, took four years.

Writing quickly may seem like a good idea, but unless you are writing so people can read, it really doesn't matter how fast your fingers flow across the keyboard. 17 days felt doable, but I allowed myself a seven-day bonus window.

As my main resources are ideas and technology, I did make sure that my brain would be well fuelled, and my technology would be working well – but always with a backup. I keep copies of everything. I also created a master set of the 17 branding. This was so I could make posts in the group, design headers for newsletters and titles for videos and do it quickly. I also ensured I knew what was happening with the back-office technology that would be needed to market, sell books and process orders. That wasn't something I wanted to be working out 12 days into the project. Prepare, prepare, prepare.

t time discussing with my small team (three of us) ie 17 project would involve and exactly what we would

I was unable to create a resource myself, I made the decisi... work with partners who could help. This freed up lots of my time to focus on developing 17 The Group and writing the book.

My record-keeping could be better, but cloud technology has enabled three of us to work on the same manuscript, link videos to websites, emails to databases and check details such as open rates, clickthroughs, 'likes' and comments to ensure we stayed on track.

I knew – from my records of other pop-up projects – when our participants were most likely to need a boost, how much time I would need to be involved and how much automation would be acceptable.

I have been demanding, but set out to do it all with a smile on my face and a soft tone in my voice. Getting quotes from printers can normally take a week; I insisted on having them the same day. When people in the 17 group made requests, Team 17 and I would answer during evenings and weekends. This is not something I would expect in the long term from myself or my team, but felt it was okay to be demanding for 17 days. We were working on a Massive Action Project.

Did it work? If you're holding a book right now, yes. If it's just me looking at screen…

At the other end of the scale to Massive Action is Little Action. Here's a list of

17 little things I do often

1 Enjoy a cup of Ringtons tea
2 Hang upside down on an inversion table
3 Make Lego models
4 Smell whisky corks
5 Laugh
6 Look at my wife and think, 'Wow, I'm punchin'
7 Ask Alexa for a joke then be disappointed by the results
8 Say I'll do something without knowing how
9 Get distracted
10 Buy a book without knowing much about its content
11 Test pens – then forget to throw out the ones that don't work
12 Jigsaw puzzles
13 Just look at my tools in my workshop
14 Read in bed
15 Forget to drink enough water
16 Have a little dance in my office
17 Write lists

17 words on
MASSIVE ACTION

You are better off taking some action than no action

Taking no action invariably leads to regret

8. 17 for Health

Let's get this bit out of the way first. I am not a health professional. All of the health advice in this chapter (and in the whole book) should only be used alongside the supervision of a doctor or other qualified health professional.

17 for health. Eat Well, Think Well, Move Well. That's it. End of chapter. Well it could be if you embrace those three areas. But let's just go a little deeper but please keep in mind this subject could be a whole book.

Eat Well

If you don't know what you should and shouldn't be eating then I can't help you. Where've you been for the last few years? There's never been more information on the right things to have in our diet, yet more people are overweight than ever. So what's happening?

There's also an increase in the number of people who join the gym, participate in Parkruns and put their bodies through all sorts of torture in an attempt to lose weight.

17

You can't out-exercise a poor diet.

Search for 15-minute healthy meals and Jamie Oliver will pop up. Everyone knows Jamie's 15-minute healthy meals actually take 17

out it's well worth it to put some quality nutrition into your
her than prick prick, nuke for four minutes on high then throw
your neck. Where's the nourishment in that?

Some folk have the strange idea that healthy food doesn't taste
good. This BS mentality ensures they keep eating the high sugar, high
salt, high carbohydrate crap that leaves them feeling lethargic.

I have a 17 challenge for you. Make a list of 17 healthy foods you
love. See if you can eat them all in one week. Get cracking now on
your list.

And now for the world's shortest advice on hydration:

Drink at least 17 litres of pure water a week.

Think Well

This whole book is about thinking well. Having a 17 mindset is all about
seeing the positive, taking action and making great things happen. But
it's not all Massive Action – sometimes we need to just slow down.

17-Minute Meditation — *Salah – 17 Rakahs daily*

Everyone knows that meditation, stilling the mind and getting into a
deeply relaxed state is good for you. The problem is, it's boring. Or at
least it **can** be boring. Even when using visualisation techniques, such
as imagining a slow-burning candle or a blossoming flower, we're soon
distracted.

Plus, what's the point? It takes years to really reap the benefits of
deep relaxation.

Or does it?

The Dalai Lama was asked how long it would take for noticeably
life-changing effects to take place through meditation. He
replied, 'Around 50 hours.'

Now that's not long in the grand scheme of things. 17 minutes a
day, a few days a week and this time next year... you're enlightened!
(Only kidding, enlighteners.)

What if you did 17 minutes twice a day, every day? You will have
experienced LIFE-CHANGING effects in a few months.

If you'd like to see a short video of how I changed my thinking
on meditation and the simple method I use, visit
www.MichaelHeppell.com/17 and take a look at Resources.

Move Well

I'd like to thank Dean Coulson, founder of The Lean Warrior, for creating this brilliant 17 Exercise Programme.

My brief to Dean was: can you develop a programme incorporating 17 exercises, using 17 reps for 17 minutes and which needs no equipment? And could you make it suitable for all fitness levels? This is what he's created for you.

Applying 17 to Your Movement

When it comes to exercise it's important to move with purpose. 17 Exercise isn't about pushing yourself so hard you walk like Robocop and take days to recover. 17 Exercise is about training intelligently and in harmony with your body. When you move with purpose always start with safety. Begin with your body's current capabilities. This minimises your chances of injury and improves your fitness, stamina, strength, agility, mobility and flexibility. This makes your body more robust and resilient for whatever life throws at you.

The 17 Exercise Programme

This is a flexible programme which can be adapted every time.

17 exercises, using 17 reps or 17 minutes.

Here are 4 ways you can use this programme…

TIMED version: All 17 exercises. 43 seconds of work then 17 seconds rest between

REPS version 1: 17 reps of each exercise, for 17 minutes. AMRAP (As Many Rounds As Possible)

REPS version 2: 17 reps of each exercise for 17 minutes (AMRAP) in reverse order

3 x AMRAP version: 5 minutes first 5 exercises, 5 minutes second 5 exercises, 7 minutes final 7 exercises (total 17 minutes)

ways make sure you warm up first. Perform the exercises
 full exercise descriptions and always seek professional
 before starting a new exercise programme.

For more information you can visit **www.michaelheppell.com/17** and go to Resources to see Dean demonstrate each of the exercises.

Here's the 17:

1 Skier Swings
2 Tuck Plank
3 Seal Jacks
4 Single Leg Bridge
5 Thoracic Reach Through

6 Squats
7 Push-Ups
8 Bird Dogs
9 High Knee Sprints
10 Table Rocks

11 Reverse Lunges
12 Renegade Rows
13 10-2s
14 Mountain Climbers
15 Y-W Holds
16 Burpees
17 Cat Camel

And here are the full descriptions of how to do them.

Skier Swings (Hinge)
Standing straight, feet hip width apart, arms by your sides. Engage your core, keep your knees soft, and maintain your spine and neck neutral and with a slight natural arch. Breathe in as you push your hips back and swing your arms back. Breathe out as you thrust your hips forward and swing your arms forward and overhead as you straighten your torso. Squeeze your glutes as you come up on your toes, and then exhale as you push your hips back and return to the starting position.

Tuck Plank (Core)
Face down on the floor, on your forearms and toes. Forearms aligned with your torso, elbows beneath your shoulders, keep your back straight, tuck your hips forward. Regression (make it easier): elevate forearms onto a step.

Seal Jacks (Locomotion)
Stand tall with feet together and arms extended in front of your chest and palms together. Jump out with your legs, feet shoulder width apart whilst drawing your arms back to the sides. Jump back to start and repeat.

Single Leg Bridge (Legs – Hinge)
Lie on your back with your legs bent at 90 degrees, feet flat on the floor and arms out by your sides. Lift your right foot towards the ceiling, whilst holding your knee above your hip. Keeping your hips level, push through your left heel and extend your hips towards the ceiling. Lower to the floor and repeat with opposite leg. Regression: keep both feet on the floor, squeeze glutes and extend your hips off the floor until you form a straight line from your knees to shoulder. Lower and repeat.

Thoracic Reach Through (Mobility)
Kneel with knees hip width apart and hands on the ground under your shoulders. Start by taking your right hand and reaching under and through the opposite arm and leg, following hand with your eyes. Draw the arm back and rotate as you extend the arm overhead in the opposite direction.

Squats (Legs)
Stand with your feet shoulder width apart, hands in front of you. Push hips back and sit as far back as you can whilst keeping your feet flat on the floor, keeping the chest up, back straight and looking forward. The key is to start the movement with your hips and descend until your upper thighs are parallel to the floor. Return to the start position. Regression: if you feel unsteady, stand next to something sturdy and use one hand to lightly support you.

Push-ups (Push)
Push-up position: arms straight down from your shoulders, perpendicular to the floor, feet hip width apart, weight on your hands and toes and body straight from shoulders to ankles. Brace your stomach and squeeze your glutes, lower chest towards the floor. Push back to start position. Regression: elevate hands on a step or chair, maintain good form.

Bird Dogs (Core)

Kneel with knees hip width apart and hands on the ground under your shoulders. Brace your stomach, with your back flat, extend your right arm and opposite leg whilst maintaining balance, keeping your hips square to the ground, maintaining a straight back. Return hand and knee to the floor and repeat with opposite limbs. Regression: if your back begins to sag, start by lifting arm and leg a few inches from the ground and increase as you feel more confident in maintaining a straight back.

High Knee Sprints (Locomotion)

Standing feet hip width apart, start by running on the spot, bringing opposite arm and knee up at the same time, bringing your knees as high as you can. Regression: instead of running on the spot, march instead with torso upright and knees high.

Table Rocks (Mobility)

Begin seated on the ground, knees bent, with your feet flat on the floor. Place your hands underneath your shoulders, fingers pointing straight back. Start by pinching your shoulder blades together (retract), and press your hips high. Reach a flat body position where your hips are in line with your shoulders and knees. Keep your neck neutral by looking overhead. Be sure your elbows remain straight and your shoulder blades stay retracted. Briefly hold the top position before lowering your hips back to the floor. Regression: hold the top position (hips up) for the duration of the exercise.

Reverse Lunges (Legs)

Start feet hip width apart. Take a long step back with your right foot until the top of your left thigh is parallel to the floor and your right knee almost touching the floor. Keep your torso upright. Step back to start position and repeat with the other leg. Regression: if you feel unsteady, stand next to something sturdy and use for support.

Renegade Rows (Pull)

Set up as you would for a push-up, with feet shoulder width apart and shoulders over hands. Tuck hips forward and squeeze your glutes. Brace stomach then lift right hand from the floor, bringing your elbow as far back as you can whilst keeping your hips flat (do not twist your torso). Return hand to the floor and repeat on the other side. Regression: elevate hands onto step or other solid surface.

10-2s (Core)
Stand tall with feet shoulder width apart, arms extended in front of your chest and palms together. Keeping your hips static (resist the twist) and torso upright, turn your torso so your hands are in the 10 o'clock position, then rotate the opposite way to the 2 o'clock position. Repeat as fast as you can whilst maintaining proper form.

Mountain Climbers (Locomotion + Core)
Set up as you would for a push-up. Bring one knee forward towards your chest and return to start position before repeating with other knee. Work at increasing your speed. Regression: elevate hands onto step or other solid surface.

Y-W Holds (Mobility)
Lie on your front with your hands by your shoulders. Begin by pinching (retracting) your shoulder blades, lift your hands off the floor and pull your elbows towards your sides (W position). From here, extend your arms forward and away from your body/head (Y position), and keep your head/spine neutral by looking at the floor. Repeat movement whilst keeping shoulders retracted. Regression: instead of performing the exercise on your front, change to a tall kneeling position.

Burpees (Locomotion)
Stand with feet hip width apart, squat down and put your hands on the floor outside your feet, kick your legs backward so you are in a push-up position. Pull your feet back in and jump up with arms overhead. Land and repeat. Regression: elevate your hand position on a step and either kick your feet back or step, bring forward and stand.

Cat Camel (Mobility)
Kneel on all fours with your hands under your shoulders and your knees under your hips. Keep your elbows straight, look up toward the ceiling, and arch your back as much as is comfortable. Pause momentarily, tuck your chin, and round your back. During the arch (cat), pinch your shoulder blades together. During the curl (camel), spread your shoulder blades apart and pull the middle of your back strongly upward. Keep your neck in line with the rest of your spine.

HEALTH
in 17 words

Impacts the whole

The single most important thing you can work on

It is everything

Your health

9. Get Back in the Saddle

The expression has been around for thousands of years. Well, since horses had saddles.

17 is not about having 17 highly successful, perfect, brilliant days – it's about your intent.

I have huge respect for anybody who has a wobble, messes up. BUT then gets back on it. We can all do that – because we are human. And today is the best day to re-engage. To help you get back in the saddle, or stay in the saddle or simply to adjust yourself in the saddle – the metaphorical saddle – to avoid quitting and to get stuff done.

Here are 17 ways to help you get back in the saddle...

1. Make a Public Post - do it on a social media platform
I know social media can get a hard rub at times but it's interesting that when you do post something, and it comes from the right place, you receive encouragement and support. This was really evident in the 17 pop-up group, where members would share how they'd fallen out of the saddle. Immediately, others gave them words of encouragement and support. At the end of the day, people are good.

2. Support Someone Else
By supporting other people it's wonderful how you feel supported yourself. It's true that when you're encouraged you feel good. But giving support feels great.

t That You Will Fall Off

_very person who has learned to ride has – it's okay.

I remember the first time I rode a horse. I was absolutely terrified. The sheer size of the thing. Okay, so it was Scarborough and that horse was a seaside donkey, but honestly it was huge – I was three.

My friend Justine used to ride thoroughbred racehorses. Her dad, Stan, was a champion jockey who'd won the Cheltenham Gold Cup. I remember one day watching the Grand National with Justine, her dad and the family. Stan gave a complete step-by-step, blow-by-blow commentary of the whole race. And did it from the viewpoint of a jockey.

At one point there was a terrible accident. Riders, horses, fences were everywhere. We gasped! Stan identified who'd fallen before the commentator, and at the end of the race everybody gave an opinion of what happened.

I asked Stan what happens when you fall off. He looked at me (like I'd just fallen off a horse) and in the calmest voice he said, 'You get back on. You see, Michael, that's what riding horses is about.'

4. Create a Shortlist

A shortlist of things you have achieved – and I mean anything. Now look at it.

Okay, I know you haven't written it yet because you're reading the book and not writing things down, but I would suggest that you take a few moments after you've read this chapter to write a list of the things that you **have** achieved.

Keep it in a safe place. Maybe have it in the Notes section on your phone. Then you can access it at any time. Especially when you feel like you're falling out of the saddle. It's your instant boost.

17

In case of a self-doubt emergency – break glass and read list.

The secret is to write it now when you don't need it, so it's there when you do.

5. Visualise a Hyper-Short-term Future

So often when people visualise their futures, they are looking to a time long into the coming months, years and sometimes decades. How about creating a hyper-short-term future?

What will 24 hours from now look like? 24 hours from when you got back in the saddle and did something? Anything.

By taking a few moments to visualise exactly where you want to be in the hyper-short term (I've even done this for an hour from now), you'll be amazed at how much positive change you feel right now.

6. Create a Reward System for Yourself

How will you reward yourself (the most important person in the world) when you have completed a challenge? My wife, Christine, had a wonderful way to get through her tasks at work. She would line up sweets on the top of her keyboard and only allow herself one if she completed a task. This simple reward system became a game. Making challenges fun and gamifying the tasks is an easier way to get back in the saddle.

7. Consider Something You Can Use to Avoid Pain

Gaining pleasure is undoubtedly a strong motivator. Avoiding pain is stronger. We sometimes need to avoid pain to get off our backsides and try again. Consider the humiliation of not getting back in the saddle and completing what you set out to do. Imagine a parent encouraging a child to do something, only for the child to turn to their parent and say, 'Well you quit.' Ouch!

A word of warning: avoiding pain is a good short-term motivator but I wouldn't recommend it for long-term motivation.

8. Double Up

Maybe your goal just isn't exciting enough. Is there something you could do to stretch yourself even further? If you were going to write 500 words a day but aren't achieving it, what would you need to get back in the saddle?

you step it up to 1,000 words? Challenge yourself. Get out of nfort zone and get it done. Sometimes you need to be pushed a little more to make you take action.

9. Stop, Start, Keep

I love Stop, Start, Keep as a way of gathering feedback from colleagues. What would you like to Stop doing, Start doing and Keep doing?

Maybe it's a good question to ask yourself to give you enough reasons to get back in the saddle. Imagine you have a 17 goal to lose some weight and improve your overall level of fitness. You realise you've had two days where you were out of the saddle.

Ask yourself the three questions. What am I going to stop doing? Stop eating between meals when you get a dose of the snack attacks. What are you going to start doing? Taking exercise is going to make a huge difference, but just thinking about it makes no difference at all. Start today. And finally what are you going to keep doing? You're going to keep your goal, keep your great attitude, keep drinking glasses of water, keep getting eight hours' sleep.

10. Breathe

Slow down. Consider a visit to White Island. White Island is my own relaxation and mental programming audio series.[9] There are loads of options out there from Headspace to Calm. They all have the same basic premise. By slowing down, breathing properly and experiencing a guided visualisation, you will slow down your thinking and gift yourself the benefit of a mental reset.

11. Create a Visual Image

Design a strong visual image of you achieving what you need to achieve. Print it. Stick it everywhere. I'm no fan of 'cosmic ordering' and really do believe you need to do a little more than just hope for an outcome and let the universe do its thing. However, I am passionate about creating visual images as a driver to help you achieve your goals. When you see an image of the goal several times a day it helps you to make better decisions and take correct actions.

---

[9] White Island also helps with sleep, goal setting and positivity. You can find out more at **www.michaelheppell.com/17**

12. Use Affirmations

Alongside great visuals come affirmations. Choosing powerful words that intensely motivate you is a great way to get you focused, halt a negative spiral and replace it with a positive one. My favourite is: 'Do it now. Do it now! DO IT NOW!' I use it when I find myself procrastinating. After the first 'do it now' I can already feel myself taking action and by the third, I'm on it.

13. Set a Mid-Term Goal

Ask yourself, 'How will I feel at the end of 17 when I've achieved my 17 goal in a week, two weeks or in a few days?'

Once you understand the outcome, take a moment to See It, Hear It, Feel It. Go deep. Add colour. Intensify the feelings. If you can, add smell, taste and touch. The more vivid you can make this scenario the better.

14. Release the Past with Joy

It's gone. There is only now. When I first read *The Power of Now* by Eckhart Tolle (published by Yellow Kite) it took me a while to get my head around the concept. No past. No future. Only now. I won't attempt to explain it in one paragraph other than: once you accept that the past really has gone it is so much easier to accept the present as it is and consider the future to be unknown and outside of your control.

15. Give Yourself 17 Reasons Why It's a Must

You probably won't be able to do this. It's really hard to write 17 different reasons to do anything. But by aiming to write 17, I bet you can write way more than five. See '17 in Lists' on page 77 for more ideas on writing lists.

16. 'Now I am back in the saddle...'

Write those words, 'Now I am back in the saddle...' and complete the rest of the sentence. There is something quite wonderful about writing things down. Hopefully you will have a notepad next to you now as there is something even more special about physically writing something with pen and paper rather than using the notes section of your phone.

t saying this as an old fuddy-duddy (at the time of writing I'm
se my phone for almost everything else. But nothing beats
notepad and pen for taking notes.

17. You've Got This

And after all of this, just know that I know you've got this. Giddy up.
Yeeehaaaa!

Whenever I need a boost, I find music is the ultimate spark. I know we
all have our own tastes, but...

17 albums I think you must listen to (but probably won't)

1   *Super* – Pet Shop Boys
2   *Diamonds and Pearls* – Prince
3   *Random Access Memories* – Daft Punk
4   *Family Dinner Vol 1* – Snarky Puppy
5   *Some Nights* – Fun.
6   *Geography* – Tom Misch
7   *Listen without Prejudice* – George Michael
8   *Rumours* – Fleetwood Mac
9   *A Night at the Opera* – Queen
10 *Out of the Blue* – Electric Light Orchestra
11 *Purple Electric Violin Concerto* – Ed Alleyne-Johnson
12 *Tubular Bells II* – Mike Oldfield
13 *No.1 In Heaven* – Sparks
14 *Mad, Bad and Dangerous to Know* – Dead or Alive
15 *Love and Dancing* – The (Human) League, Unlimited
    Orchestra
16 *Flaunt It* – Sigue Sigue Sputnik
17 *Race for Space* – Public Service Broadcasting

17 words on RESTARTING

When the going gets tough

The tough get off their sorry backsides and back in the saddle

10. The Deep Think

'What were you thinking?'

'Ermm, nothing.'

Ever had that conversation? Have you found yourself saying 'Eeeh, I haven't got time to think'? Okay, maybe without the 'Eeeh'.

Just normal thinking time is seen as a luxury. Something for later – for 'When I get a minute'. Deep Thinking time is put off for years; stored up for that 'once-in-a-lifetime visit to the Peruvian foothills' but only after the selfie.

You most likely don't spend enough (or any) time thinking. I don't mean meditating. Fling a flip-flop into the air and the chances are it'll land on someone banging on about how important it is to meditate. (I know, I'm one of them.)

I mean thinking. **Deep Thinking.**

Here's how you do it:

> Sit somewhere quiet
>
> Do your best not to be disturbed
>
> Start to think
>
> No distractions. No music. No notepad.
>
> Just you and your thoughts
>
> For 17 minutes.

You can do it today.

When we held the 17 pop-up group, I hosted The Big Think. Participants from 17 different countries (couldn't have planned that) came together for 17 minutes of Deep Thinking. And we did it on Zoom.

Here's what some people said.

'Wow. I've never done that before, but I want to do it again.'

'I really enjoyed having the freedom to let my mind chatter and found some real nuggets emerged as part of the process.'

'It feels like a counterbalance to meditation.'

'Deeply profound, I found tears flowing.'

'I felt very very connected to others.'

'I had so many amazing ideas. Loved it.'

I love the idea of the discipline. And I love the idea of the unruliness of a deep-thinking mind. Where will it end up?

Afterwards you can share your experiences. Or just take time to consider your own 17 minutes of Deep Thinking.

17 things to Deep Think about for 17 minutes

1 Reasons to be cheerful

2 Places you've been

3 Friends from school

4 Current friends

5 Places you would like to go

6 Things that make you laugh

7 Places you've been

8 Quotes that motivate you

9 Favourite items of clothing from your wardrobe

10 Things you wish you hadn't done

11 Things you're glad you have done

12 Things you would like to do

13 Where you will be in 17 years

14 Where you will be in 17 months

15 Useful information you learned at school

16 Advice to give your younger self (that you could probably take now)

17 Go through the alphabet and for each letter just consider the first thing that comes to mind. Think on this for 30 seconds at a time.

17 words on
DEEP THINKING

Think

Think harder

Try to stop your thinking

Just let the thinking happen

Now you are thinking

11. 17 in Lists

Most people write lists of ten. 17 makes you think a little harder. When Jeffrey Gitomer read my newsletter about 17 lists he commented that he was completely taken off track and into another place. He messaged me: 'Michael, lists make you think, make you remember and make you smile.'

> 17
>
> **'Lists make you think, make you remember and make you smile.'**

He also suggested more lists for my list of lists.

This is a different chapter. As well as the lists interspersed throughout this book, this is a chapter of lists. Some I've populated with my thinking and some are just a heading waiting to be completed.

Read mine, conclude your own, add, chop, change – do what you like, just make sure you stretch yourself to 17. All the thinking, benefits and fun are in you coming up with the last seven items of your lists.

le I know and admire who you probably won't have heard of. Or have you?

1 Andy Alderson
2 Vanessa Thompson
3 Fiona Deal
4 Dorothy Tilney
5 Jamie Waller
6 Sara Cox
7 Walter Riddell
8 Sarah Stonehouse
9 Gillian Neish
10 Gavin Sewell
11 Sarah Heppell
12 Irene Dorner
13 Tim Brownson
14 Helen Gosney
15 Lisa Raisbeck
16 Richard Nugent
17 Dr Guillermo Recatero Rude

17 of my favourite places to stay

1 Home
2 Nobu, Marbella
3 Shutters on the Beach, Santa Monica
4 Luton Hoo
5 Pure Salt, Garonda
6 ME
7 Gleneagles
8 The Traddock, Austwick
9 Old Government House, Guernsey
10 Hotel 41, London
11 Bahia del Duque, Tenerife
12 Milestone, Kensington
13 Ushuaïa, Ibiza
14 Ritz Carlton, Singapore
15 Beverly Wiltshire, Los Angeles
16 Portmarnock Resort, Dublin
17 Kestrel

17 movies I love to watch

1 *The Castle*
2 *Inside Man*
3 *Pulp Fiction*
4 *Bohemian Rhapsody*
5 *Ferris Bueller's Day Off*
6 *Mission: Impossible*
7 *Cinema Paradiso*
8 *The Rocky Horror Picture Show*
9 *Kes*
10 *Back to the Future*
11 *Love Actually*
12 *Toy Story*
13 *The Grinch*
14 *LA Story*
15 *Top Gun*
16 *Home Alone*
17 *It's a Wonderful Life*

17 things I remember from being a kid (some that we don't have now)

1 Marathon chocolate bars
2 Rear car seats with no seatbelts
3 Rope swings
4 Your own VHS video tape
5 Three TV channels and the excitement of Channel 4
6 Recording the charts on a Sunday
7 Cresta – the stickiest most e-numbered pop of all time
8 Walking – everywhere
9 Being allowed on 'The Big Field' at school
10 Coming home cos we heard the whistle
11 Queuing to buy tickets from a box office
12 People smoking on buses and planes
13 Waiting to use the phone
14 'Backing' schoolbooks
15 That machine at Clarks that measured (crushed) your feet
16 The Sunday night dread of going to school
17 Dial-a-disc

I appreciate this list is very UK biased. What do you remember?

17 ways to feel momentarily magic

1 Smile
2 Force a laugh – do this for 30 seconds
3 Look at one small thing of beauty
4 Make a wish
5 Stare out of the window
6 Drink a big glass of water
7 Finish something
8 Start something
9 Moisturise
10 Delete a bunch of emails
11 Make something from scratch
12 See that the car is fully fuelled
13 Wave at a neighbour
14 Wake up
15 Put your head back in the shower – let the water hit your face
16 Complete your workout
17 Read something new

17 emails I always open and people I follow

1 Paul Mort – Daily emails
2 Tim Brownson – Amazing Blog
3 @FatTony – Instagram
4 @ThisIsDavina – Twitter and Insta
5 @fly276 KCMoi – Twitter
6 Richard Nugent, Twenty One Leadership – email, LinkedIn and Twitter
7 Andy Alderson Vanarama – LinkedIn
8 @AndyWoodturner – Twitter
9 @SarahHeppellPR – Twitter and Insta
10 Tom Peters – Email and Twitter
11 @JonathanRaggett – Twitter
12 Andy Bounds – LinkedIn
13 Liz Heppell – email
14 @TheSumoGuy – Twitter
15 @TerryLaybourne – Twitter and Insta
16 Seth Godin – Daily blog email
17 Christine Heppell – Text and WhatsApp

And here are 17 more to contemplate and complete

17 characteristics of success

17 characteristics of failure

17 books you could read again

17 happiest memories

17 CDs (or vinyls) you could never throw out

17 things that make me laugh out loud

17 people I would like to meet

17 biggest regrets

17 friends I remember from being 1 to 17

17 items I couldn't live without

17 ways I can save money

17 questions I like to answer

17 greatest TV shows

17 places I must visit

17 books I have yet to read

17 things I would like to quit

17 things I would like to start

12. 17 Stories from 17

When 17 was created, it launched with a pop-up group. I shared ideas and created a 17-day community. We had hundreds of achievements and stories, each person sharing their own 17 successes; some large, some small.

Here are 17 stories we hope will inspire you. You can read more at **www.michaelheppell.com/17**

New Start – Jessica Ching

If it wasn't for 17, I wouldn't have had the courage tell my employer that I'd like to leave.

I'd been unhappy with my career for a long while, never really feeling a part of it and it was leading me down a dark path (mentally). Then 17 came along and I was instantly connected to the concept. The Team 17 people in the group gave me such encouragement and shared some lovely stories, along with the inspirational live chats by Michael. So I thought:

'What the hell! I need to be happy, I want to be happy. I need to do something I love.'

And that's what I'm doing. I've taken the bull by the horns and I am going to be an interior designer. I've enrolled on a design course, I've reached out to interior designers local to me for advice and I'm going to find a part-time job to keep me going while I retrain.

This is a new and scary start for me but one I wish I had done two decades ago.

17lbs in 17 Days – Sarah Patton

I wanted to be healthier as well as lose some weight for an operation. Prior to 17 I couldn't seem to get my act together.

I hated exercise, but using 17 I'm inspired to tackle things. I see daily tasks in manageable achievable chunks of 17-Minute Sprints. Or for bigger challenges over 17 hours or 17 days! Having finally taken hold of my life by the short and curlies and given it a damn good shake-up I have stopped procrastinating about heaps of 'stuff'.

I gave up sugar and bread and started exercising daily. By day 7 I had lost 3 kg (6.6 lbs), by day 13 I'd lost a total of 6.5 kgs (14 lbs) and by day 17 it was 8 kg – that's 17.6 lbs!

I'm dancing to 17 random tunes a day and, yes, I dance like no one's watching. I've been decluttering my life by donating 17 items a day to charity and allowing at least 17 minutes a day to meditate and be thankful.

I've noticed I am laughing and smiling more. I feel more present in my own life and I've been more present for others too. I am deliberately going out of my way to smile at strangers because I want to pass on the positive effects of 17. I now see and hear '17' popping up everywhere from social media to songs on the radio!

17-Minute Windows – Ladey Adey

It's easy to waste a spare 17 minutes, just waiting for the next thing to occur; perhaps wander around, make a cup of coffee, think about the next meeting, look at a couple of emails, visit social media and then suddenly... the time has gone.

17 has made me re-evaluate those 17-minute windows. It might be that I continue a project, adding a little more to it to progress it. I can add to a report or a piece of writing. Those which always seem too big to do in one go. The one I've been procrastinating about.

Claiming back the odd 17 minutes here and there has become significant to me and the 17 Challenge has raised my awareness of time. And 17 is a lovely number which is often the number of minutes I have between calls or between meetings.

Random 17s – Ian Pearson

It's such a random number, 17, and because of this I undertook 17 random acts over 17 days.

My starting point was to move along a wartime ration diet writing project which had, coincidentally, stalled at 17,000 words. Random act number one: cooking the 17th dish from a wartime recipe book – Carrot jam (tastes like jam, very orange).

But even that was too structured, so among other ideas I:
- Practised showering and washing my hair in less than 1.7 minutes (easy 58 seconds).
- Took 17 random photos on my early morning walk.
- Had 17-minute walks to test St Augustine's 'solvitur ambulando' theory (it is solved by walking).
- Wrote a virtual quiz with all the answers being related to 17. (Who are the boyband named after the postcode for Walthamstow?)
- Wrote a 17-syllable haiku (Heppell inspires, Just seventeen seconds, To scribble this haiku).
- Created the 17-minute meeting.
- And probably the least sensible and most unstructured: managed to consume 17 units of alcohol in one day.

Flipping the Guilt – David Rogers

A couple of weeks into lockdown we unfortunately lost one of our dogs through ill health. Whilst it was a very upsetting time for my wife and I, we were able to spend time talking about our grief, and how I had been able to spend all day every day with him over the previous two weeks as I was working from home.

I started to reflect on the positive impact the lockdown was having on me; I was exercising regularly, eating healthily, reading and working on my personal development.

Then the guilt hit me. Why should I be feeling so positive about everything? After all, there are families losing loved ones and not able to see them in hospital at the time – how could I be so insensitive?

I wrote about it in the 17 group and the support I received, telling me that it wasn't a bad thing and that it could turn into something really positive, made me want to give something back.

17 gave me that opportunity. I was keen to share some of the positive actions I had taken, so I committed to sharing 17 great recipes and 17 fitness workouts. Even if this inspired one person to comment or take action I will have had a positive impact on someone's life. And that is all I want to have: a positive impact.

Hedging – Lucy Kendall

When the wind picks up, litter blows into my garden from the street. It drives me crackers. Do you know what would sort that out? A hedge!

In April 2016, I was given the keys to my new home. I loved it. One of the first things I wanted to do was plant a hedge. Then life got in the way. Don't get me wrong, I did lots of things but every time I walked through the front door, I looked at my neighbour's beautiful hedge and thought, 'I want a hedge!'

Still I didn't find the time. I'd convinced myself it was too big a job. Besides, I had other things to do and it was going to be hard.

Then I discovered 17. My newfound knowledge of what is possible in a mere 17 minutes gave me an idea. It was a sunny Saturday (July 2020 – four years and four months since I decided I wanted a hedge) and I was sick of not having a hedge.

I set my timer for 17 minutes, grabbed a spade and went for it. I managed to dig a bed for my hedge, and it took me exactly... 17 minutes. Something that I wanted for over four years took me only 17 minutes to start. The plants arrive this week and I think after two 17-Minute Sprints I'll have my hedge.

17 in Grief – Fiona Setch

2 May 2020 was the day my darling Mum chose to die.

Yes, she was a statistic the news bulletins featured, one of the 366 people in England who had died of coronavirus that day.

I had to say goodbye to my darling Mum through her nursing home window, singing 'Lord of the Dance' to her through a small opening and telling her how much we loved her.

In my previous career as a nurse, I had cared for dying patients and know that even when our loved ones have lapsed into unconsciousness, holding their hands and talking to them is important. Touch and hearing are the senses that are still present.

But I couldn't do either. After being her carer for 22 years, this was not the way we were meant to say goodbye. Six weeks of watching her through her window.

I wanted to use 17 to do so much. My long list of possibilities included: making a different soup every day, litter picking, throwing 17 balls for Millie, writing cards to say thank you, being a brilliant wife, being a brilliant mum, exercising, developing my writing, hoovering. To be busy with a capital B!

And after four days I had to stop. It hit me like a brick wall...

I wrote a poem, cancelled the next couple of hours and I realised what I needed to do. Each day would be to gift myself. 17 minutes of being with my grief... thinking about Mum, my loss and crying.

That's what I've done every day... breathed in and thought about my darling Mum. Sometimes I smile, sometimes I cry. 17 has given me permission to be with my loss.

Saturday 4th July, good morning all
Been for a walk and hit a brick wall
Only been 8 weeks since Mum died
For 17 minutes – oh how I've cried
I need to give my head some space
How my heart longs to see her face
My darling Mum I miss your 'wow'
Your dementia made me pause
to be in your now
Life's yin and yang: sweet sadness too
Today I give myself permission to be blue

An Unusual 17 Commute – Sally Betts

I decided to complete 17 tiny habits a day for 17 days with a hope they'd become my normal.

The tricky bits. Remembering to do them. Such as putting a load in the washing machine so I could hang it out to dry before 3pm and finding the motivation. I came up with this crazy idea to commute to work on my bike. I work from home. So I used my exercise bike!

I linked my new habits to things I do anyway. For some, I 'habit stacked', linking one new habit to another. When I made my first cup of coffee, I'd unload the dishwasher. Unloading the dishwasher triggered checking how full the laundry basket was. I added: take a moment to look out of the window too.

The number 17 acted as my motivator; soon I cycled for 17 minutes while planning my day – in 17-minute slots of course! And I have the aspiration to be in the top 17% of education consultants.

Pipe Up! – Nicholas Irwin

Aged 12 the doctor suggested to my worried mum that 'Expanding my lungs would help my asthma'. I was promptly dispatched to a local band to learn the bagpipes.

In my mid 20s, after 14 years' playing, attending contests, parades, events, etc, I decided that I had had enough and packed my pipes away for the last time.

Fast forward to 2018. I was looking for a challenge. A new skill that I could learn. Something recreational that I would enjoy doing. But wasn't sure what I could do.

Then one evening my interest was piqued when I searched, 'bagpipes' on eBay. £460 later and I was the proud owner of a set of second-hand 'Smallpipes' complete with a 'free case'. Then the worry started. The photos look okay, but will they be fully complete? How difficult will they be to play? They have bellows!

When the pipes arrived, they needed some setting up. It took a bit of time; the bellows were awkward to operate but I tinkered. Then put them away. They came out less and less. They went from sitting room to a spare bedroom, and soon I was hardly bringing them out at all.

Then the 17 Challenge came along. Time for action. My target was to spend at least 17 minutes per day for 17 days. At the end of the Challenge I would be able to operate the pipes effectively and be able to play at least seven tunes to a reasonable standard and ten other tunes partially.

17 days later – target achieved.

17 Days Sugar Free – Sheila Starr

When I was young, my sister would spend her 50p pocket money on a magazine, and I'd fill my paper bag with 100 halfpenny sweets. Yes, I would call myself a sugar addict. I have always loved eating sweeties and chocolate. Some people drink a glass of wine while they cook, I'll munch on Smarties.

I'd buy the three for £1 chocolate bars to eat over three days, then eat them all in ten minutes. Luckily, I don't have a weight problem – just a sugar habit.

I decided to go 17 days with no sugar. No biscuits, chocolate, cake or sweets. How hard could it be? Very! But the support was amazing, and I was able to find swaps. Yes, I chose healthy snacks. With 17 I was held to account, congratulated and able to help and inspire others with my success.

17 days is an achievable target. I did it.

On day 18? I celebrated with a big sticky Belgian bun. But then I went on to do another 17 days of no sugar. I'd proven I can.

Running and Writing with 17 – Nick Finney

17 helped me in two key ways. Writing and keeping fit.

I'm a member of Michael's 'Write That Book Masterclass'. The thought of putting 30,000-plus words down on paper was, to say the least, daunting. But using the 17-Minute Sprint technique worked amazingly well. 17 minutes is not long enough to feel inconvenienced, but neither is it so short that you can't make progress. Many times I sat for one sprint and ended up adding another. With the extra motivation, I completed the first draft of my story during my 17-day challenge.

For fitness... I'd been suffering from a variety of running injuries. I used 17 to flip my running; rather than set myself a distance to run, I started to see how far I could go in 17 minutes. No more, no less. By limiting the time, I reduced my chances of overdoing things, but I still gave myself a target to aim for.

17 The Switch – Des Reynolds

Through the first half of 17 I had been concentrating on 17 minutes of exercise, 17 reading challenges a day plus 17 minutes' coaching practice. Then on 8 July I was told that my contract, which ends in September, was unlikely to be extended.

Part 2! I instantly switched my 17 coaching focus and started to use 17 thinking to coach myself. I thought of 17 people to contact and created a list of 17 different places to look for new roles.

I took Massive Action and one action I carried out immediately caused some of my senior managers to look at ways to keep me.

17 has truly taught an already positive person the benefits of short bursts of action with definite goals.

Double the Work, Twice the Effectiveness – Lynton Lomas
I started 17 with my job under consultation. Although I was one of the fortunate ones, I lost two friends and colleagues and my personal workload doubled overnight. This was at the same time as learning, tweaking, and creating a whole new virtual sales journey for my customers.

I design and sell kitchens and bathrooms, so it's no small task. By using 17-Minute Sprints to create new scripts, ways of working etc sales are flying in. I'm loving it.

The added bonus is knowing I'm part of a fantastic community of positive like-minded people using 17. It makes this a whole lot easier.

Delete Delete – Angela Vale
I had this mammoth (to me) task of deleting some of the nearly 9,010 photos on my phone. I needed to free up space but this was such an onerous job I kept putting it off.

Then up pops 17 like a knight in shining armour with a brilliant 17 concept. Do whatever you wish in sprints of 17 minutes for 17 days. So I decided to delete photographs.

I set my timer each morning for 17 minutes, started deleting and 'hey presto' the job was being done. Not just done but smashed. I deleted 5,212 in 17 days.

17 achievements can be large or small, but with such a simple and effective idea, it just happens. I guarantee you will use 17 for the rest of your life… I know I will.

17 Book Mountain – Jacqueline Shaw
I looked at the books I'd set aside and suddenly felt a determination. It was time to read them. I always used the excuse of never finding the time or being too tired to read. That's how I ended up with a stack of unread books. Motivated by 17, I set my target of reading. My plan was 17 x 3. I chose to read in the morning, afternoon and evening. I manged eight books from my pile.

This new thinking was challenged by my desire to allow me more time for myself (ME time), as I've always helped others first.

My ultimate goal was to start being kinder to myself. Now at the end of my day, I channel my energy to develop self-compassion by writing a love letter to myself.

Be a Little More Fairy – Melanie Wellard
I had no experience of social media, email promotion or online marketing; but I was determined to learn. This was my 17 challenge. I was starting my challenge from ground zero. But as I'm writing a book called The Fairy Who Could Not Quit, I knew I'd have to 'build my tribe' to sell it.

I started by creating a Facebook page and group: 'How to Be a Little More Fairy'. Which was promptly deleted three times. I couldn't decide on the name of the page, group or whether to write under a pseudonym. But I had a 17 target to post something inspirational every day. My daily 6am (sometimes 4am) task was to design and post on every possible relevant site, including my own.

I actually woke every morning excited about finding different ways of designing and portraying a message. I loved it. I experimented and played with design and I created and created. During my 17 Challenge two of my posts exceeded 500 responses.

The 17 challenge reignited my passion and creativity, which I thought had died in me after years in a soulless job. 17 has affected my life in a very profound way. It has given me back my hope and my confidence in myself.

Freelance Copywriter or Lego Set Designer? – Jenny Williams

Not that long ago, I came to the uncomfortable realisation that I'd spent almost a decade working in a job that I didn't particularly like. Not only did I not enjoy the work but there was little opportunity to develop the role. Even worse, I'd recently spent some time analysing my values and discovered that the job I'd been doing for so long didn't match ANY of them! It was clear that I must make a change, and SOON. But I felt stuck.

I'm 48 and still had absolutely no idea what I wanted to be when I 'grew up'. I challenged myself to come up with 17 different job or business ideas, every day for 17 days. No filter or analysis; everything that popped into my head went down in the notebook. After that I was a lot less blocked for ideas – in fact I had 289 options to choose from!

Next was to narrow this huge list down to just 17, choosing a mix of sensible things and others that seemed ridiculous but intriguing. I then ranked these against 17 criteria reflecting my strengths, values and what I ultimately want out of my working life, to see which of the ideas merited further investigation.

I'm still not sure whether I'll end up as a freelance copywriter, Lego set designer or something else entirely, but I'm excited to find out!

17 to Fight Back – Mark Fleming

My son Charlie was sick with leukaemia for nine months before he sadly died in 2006. It hit me hard. I suffered from depression, saw a psychiatrist and a therapist before I gradually got things back on track.

Then I lost my job – twice. In 2007 and again in 2011 and I suffered more setbacks.

Reading and listening to Michael has helped me work my way out of the maze. His books Flip It and How to Be Brilliant were instrumental in helping me tackle some mental health problems. Michael's positivity and enthusiasm shines through. His advice and tips are priceless.

This year he has been there for me again. 17 came shortly after my mother died of Covid-19 in May. There was a danger that old bad habits could resurface and knock me sideways; but Michael's puppy-like enthusiasm about his new project 17 caught my eye. So, I joined in. The positive energy and generous support was something else. 17 helps me to focus in the now and on being brilliant – not to dwell on what I have lost. Thank you, Michael.

I'd love to know your 17 stories. Please email them to hello@michaelheppell.com

17 words on STORIES

Your earliest memories

Your greatest movies

Your best times with friends

Your favourite books

Your deepest emotions

Thank You

Thank you to the incredible team who helped to create *17 The Book* in record time.

Christine Heppell – my co-writer, harshest critic, biggest cheerleader, editor and without doubt the most patient partner in the world.

Vanessa Thompson – our Third Musketeer who tirelessly looks after our customers, organises my crazy schedule and appears to be omnipresent in every project.

Sue Richardson, The Right Book Company – who greased the wheels, trusted me entirely, made the introductions and never once complained when I moved the boundaries.

Paul East, The Right Book Company – the king of book marketing and promotion who inspires me to do better with every conversation.

Lisa Johnson – for teaching me how to build an online tribe and for not telling me how hard it would be.

Clare Purkiss – the queen of virtual wiring. Thank you for sharing your secrets and giving me the confidence to connect.

The Members of my Write That Book Masterclass – thank you for your inspiration and support of a sometimes very tough teacher. But especially thank you for the kick I needed to do this.

Andrew Chapman – who edited, designed and typeset *17*. If you found this book a pleasure to read, it was down to him.

Thank You

And a huge thank you to these amazing people who made the 17 pop-up a truly brilliant, fun, learning and inspirational experience

Jacqueline Shaw books, shed clearing and pink hair **Julie Waldock** ...and breathe... **Kate Elder** thinking in 17-minute slots **Gillian Neish** changing the world 17 people at a time **Gillian Westlake** the Grace Jones of 17 – hoola! **Lynton Lomas** Laughing, Loving, Living **Elizabeth Chandler** our brilliant Barbadian bookkeeper **Dave Jeal** 17 mole hills – oh no! **Jeffrey Gitomer** promoting 17 LIVE every day to the world **Karin Borland** creatively smashing 17 **Michael Ashby** 6 mins and 28 secs! **Andree Currie** 17 stories with her grandson **Louise Gill** handbag cake to get back in the saddle **Audrey Holden** a Super Trouper **Karen Balmond** Alexa says '17 minutes again Karen – really?' **Angela Beeston** always looking amazing on the beach **Belinda Cheung** amazing Latin cha-cha dancer **Clare Froggatt** best selfie photographs ever **Jill Thompson** binge free **Alison Messom** 17 brilliant floral inspirations **Hatem Mousa** changing from reaction to action! **Teresa Cripps** come on The Hammers **Helen Johns** 17 reasons why we love Northern Soul **Mark Fleming** crazy golf and witty banter **Gayle Hubble** crochet queen **Tracy Taylor** Deep Thinking and being grateful **Diane Roe** doing her 17 while delegating the decking **Melanie Wellard** Fairy Queen **Tracey Moss** feeling confident with the clippers **Tracy McCarthy** finding time and making a difference **Mabella Farrer** floral photographer **Julie Bryant** 17 reasons why I love running **Jon Asquith** Super Coach **Mike Hubbard** helping mates and making a difference **Sheila Starr** from sweet tooth to sugar-free **Matthew Bird** from the land of smiles **Donna Sheavills** future brilliant cross-stitcher **David Palmer** haiku poet extraordinaire **Jennifer Sinclair** handwritten lists and cleared-up kitchens **Donna Clark** is it just me or is everyone seeing the number 17 everywhere? **Jenny Williams** it's time for changes, big changes **Dean Coulson** juggling life and wellness **Nicky Clements** kindest comments from Kent **Michala Johnson** 17 reasons why you are wonderful **Steve Dobby** the Steve Cram of Crammy **Sarah McGeough** look out for that Fabulous Flamingo Family **Mark Jenkinson** magnificent memes of Manchester **Colette Benham** may be kayaking reading this? **Debbie Homer-Davis** the brilliant Baby Lady **Vicky Leigh** mein Deutsch hat sich wirklich verbessert **Dawn Booth** motivational messenger **Richard Perry** now that's a book lover's breakfast! **Lucas Vigilante** official 17 poet and legendary lead singer of Lucas & The Maracas Three **Sally Betts** official party trailer maker for 17 – You ready? I'm ready! **Alie Calvert our** amazing Edinburgh runner

Donald McCorkindale spectacular Strontian sermons **Jillian Horan** stepping and freeing **Fiona Setch** the constant contributor – and she sings! **Helen Roylance-Trotman** queen of cakes – mmmmmmm **John Buttery** king of double up **Sarah Patton** the amazing shrinking woman – cuppa tea? **Lorraine Toner** painting walls and stones **Perry Huntley** Perry picked a peck of pickled peppers **Angela Vale** photo eraser extraordinaire **Joan Armstrong** photographing 17 beautiful locations in the real North **Steve Kelly** Proudly taking 17 into education and changing lives at Keighley College **Lynn Pearson** scan, sleep, smile, repeat **Lorraine Street** sensational squatter... sit-ups too **Pasquale Scornaienchi** SMILE – Good morning – SMILE **Victoria Wilson-Crane** So Exciting! Very Energetic Novel; The Enlightenment Ends? Never! **Mike Vaughan** stretching and beers – the perfect 17 combination. **Steve McGeough** taking push-ups to the next level with child-inspired weighting **Mike Garde** terrific tribe builder **David Birchall** putting the South Lakes on the map (thank you for the PR) **Nick Finney** that man with the mohawk **Neil Rutherford** the cautious statistician **Karen Morley-Chesworth** the Embarrassed Journo is born **Jeff Caplan** King of Shirts **Beth Cabiness** the laundry room is clean! **KC Chamberlain (Moi)** the queen of comments and enthusiasm **Kerry Crichton** the super creative Crystal Tipps **David Rogers** the ultimate contributor **Karrie-Ann Fox** the Worcester Walker **Karin Carruthers** the world's greatest smile – right there **Mark Norton** There was a bike rider from Poole, his quiz took us all back to school **Debbie Mitchell** Wine, Water and Wellness – Thermal Baths in Budapest? Yep, let's have 17 **Ladey Adey** time-travelling futuristic historian **Jennifer Flint** to wild eggs, the cabin and the many sundowners there **Maria White** todas nuestras gracias por enseñarnos español **Lorraine Linley** top encourager **Lindsey Holland** transforming Cheltenham one shovel at a time **Mary McGowan** tuning in from Canada with Willow **Diane Wyatt** up and at it 17 minutes earlier **Philippa Mathewson** updating daily from Dehli **Jacqueline Suffolk** vamos a montar a caballo niños **Andrea Ince** walks with Bobby (the dog) who thinks he's human **Jessica Ching** world class interior designer **Ian Pearson** let's make a gin with 17 botanicals **Christine Beech** there are 17 ways to cook an egg **Lucy Kendall** yoga queen and heroic hedge planter **Judith Stanton Meyer** what a 17th birthday **Chantal Wellavize** putting the human in HR **Garry Bryant** the Vikings are coming **Jeannie Duncanson** the cherry on the cake

You Want More?

If you would like more resources, videos, ideas, support, newsletters, 17 stories and a whole bunch of other stuff then visit www.MichaelHeppell.com/17

Team 17

Download your 3 free bonus chapters including 'Team 17', where you'll discover how to achieve your 17 goals even faster by using the power of team.

www.michaelheppell.com/17

The Author

Michael Heppell is the international bestselling author of six other books.

How to Be Brilliant – Change your ways in 90 days
Five Star Service – How to deliver exceptional customer service
Brilliant Life – Put a little more in, get so much more out
Flip It – How to get the best out of everything
How to Save an Hour Every Day
The Edge – How the best get better

Michael as a Speaker

Michael is described as one of the top three professional speakers in the world. He now uses his unique speaking style to provide amazing online keynotes and training events as well as speaking at conferences.

And now you can book Michael to present **17 The Keynote**.

Michael and Christine Heppell as coaches

Davina McCall described her first coaching session with Michael as 'The most life-changing hour and a half of my life'. They have coached hundreds of people to success with over 20 years in coaching, working one-to-one with those who have a desire to be brilliant.

Michael Heppell Ltd Training

Using powerful face-to-face and online learning and development tools, Michael and Christine Heppell have created a range of programmes and classes. If you want improved customer service, better communication, stronger leadership, personal effectiveness and the host of other outcomes, please arrange a call.

To find out more visit www.MichaelHeppell.com